A Little Kid From Flat River

Childhood Memories

By

Charles M. Province

Other books by Charles M. Province

Pure Patton
Patton's Proverbs
Patton's Third Army
The Unknown Patton
Patton's Punch Cards
I Was Patton's Doctor
General Walton Walker
Patton's One-Minute Messages
Tailgunner: The Leonard E. Thompson Story
Patton's Third Army in WWII (Children's Book)

Books Edited by Charles M. Province

Generalship; It's Diseases and Their Cure
By J.F.C. Fuller

Special thanks to David Mills for his permission to use the picture of *The Barn Dance* at the Grand Theater in Desloge, Missouri.

Published by
CMP Productions
cmprovince@gmail.com
http://www.pattonhq.com/cmp_productions.html

59257964

This book is dedicated to my mother,

Helen Marguerite Criteser.

A group of the neighborhood kids at the
the Flat River Royal Crown Bottling Plant,
around 1949. There's nothing like fizzy
sugar-water on a warm summer day.

Table of Contents

Introduction
How It All Started
Something's Wrong Him
The Boy With Green Teeth
The Boomerang
The Spelling Bee
King for a Day
Polio
Jesse James
Great-Great Aunt Mary
The Christmas Show at KFMO
Saying Goodbye
The Entertainer
Happy Birthday
Sunset Carson
No Sissies Allowed
Christmas With Grandma
Working On Grandpa's Farm
The Step Mother
Strange Children I Have Known
Grandma Was a Joiner
Shaking The Family Tree

Pictures of the Province Family

I'm on the left. Larry Kennedy is on the
right. I wouldn't make any sudden moves
if I were you. I've always liked the feel of
a well-machined blue-steeled weapon.

Introduction

When I started this project, it was going to be a book primarily for the benefit of my family and friends.

As things progressed, however, and I began to make mental notes to organize my thoughts and memories, I realized that these little stories might actually be something that others could read and enjoy. People might even get a chuckle out of some of them.

It's quite a departure from my customary material. Previously, I've written about Military History, World War II, the Korean War, Leadership, and General George S. Patton, Jr. I even wrote my own textbook when I was teaching Computer Science at the Community College in San Diego, California.

I also wrote a lot of User Manuals and Operations Guides for the computer systems we developed when I was working at the San Diego Union-Tribune newspaper. I worked at the paper for almost forty years.

Some of the stories in this little book may be a bit sad, but I've made every attempt to add some levity to make them palatable.

Perhaps the most valuable lesson I've learned throughout my life is that a person absolutely has to have a sense of humor. When a person begins to take things so seriously that everything becomes a matter of life and death, they're just asking for trouble.

I'll be the first to admit that there's nothing in this book that is earth shattering, epiphany invoking, nor ghastly startling. It's not something that would be written by a "celebrity" and it has nothing to do with drugs, sex, and all the other things that seem to sell books these days. As a matter of fact, it is my considered opinion that the "celebrities" who write their "tell all" books pretty much cause all of their own problems.

The stories in this book concern situations over which I had no control. All in all, I was essentially on my own as a kid and everything I learned, everything I did, and everything I've become is due to my own decisions and hard work. I've made my share of mistakes and bad decisions, but, for the most part, I think I turned out okay. As I often remark to my wife, "Not too bad for a kid from Flat River, I guess."

Simply put, these stories are about a little kid from a small town called Flat River, Missouri. It's all about growing up and learning the lessons that are supposed to prepare a person for life.

Some of the lessons I learned were hard and painful, but I got through them and I've continued my journey.

One important lesson I've learned is that life is all about bouncing back after it gives you a good poke in the nose.

As an old man writing this book, I can also tell you that old age is not for sissies.

If this little book turns out well and sells enough copies, I might write another one about my years in High School and my experiences in the Army. We'll see how it goes.

Charles M. Province
Oregon City, 2011

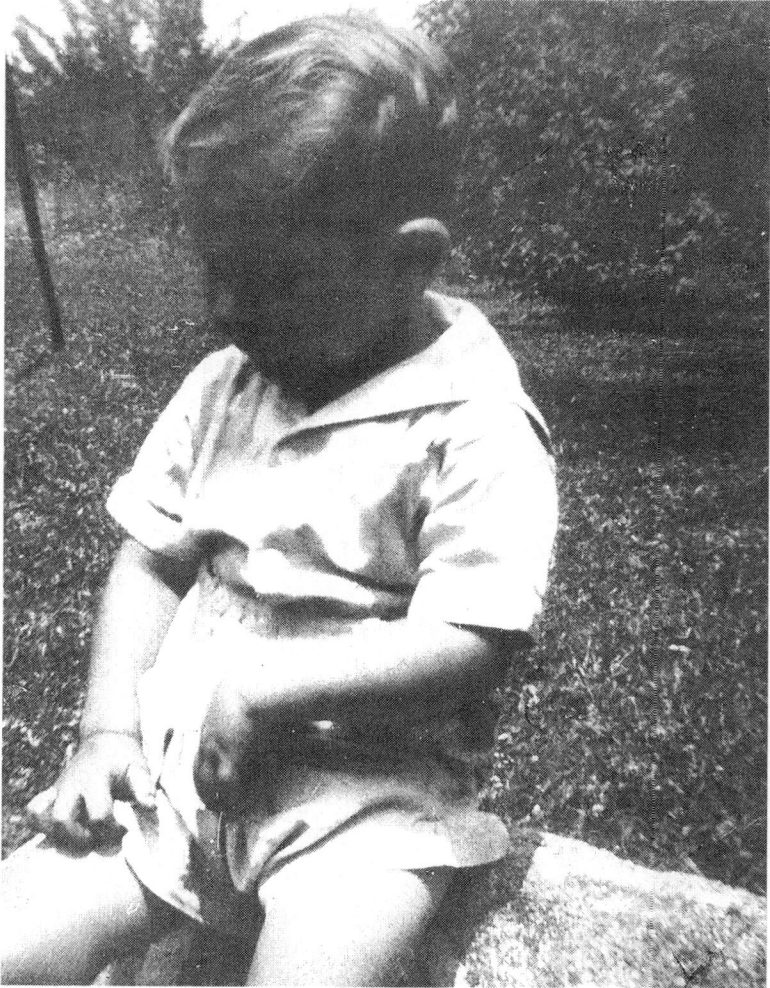

In a pensive mood.

How It All Started

I am born. That's how Charles Dickens starts his thinly disguised autobiography, David Copperfield and since Dickens is one of my favorite authors I'm going to steal that opening for this little book.

To be exact, I was born at 6:20 a.m. on the 15th of May in 1944. I was a war baby. Less than a month after my birth, the Allied invasion of Europe took place on the 6th of June, 1944. It was the last war the United States won.

The first memories I seem to have begin around three or four years of age. One of my earliest memories, however, is the bathroom that my old man built in our small house at 301 First Street in Flat River, Missouri. Mama was giving me a bath in our new bathtub and I asked her why she sat on the toilet to go potty while I could stand up. She explained things to me.

Our original house was quite small, having only two rooms. That's why the old man got it so cheap.

My old man was pretty lucky during World War II. Because he was in a "protected occupation" he was allowed to stay home and work in the mines instead of being drafted for military service. He used this to his advantage, working double shifts to bolster his weekly paycheck. With the extra money, he managed to add two additional rooms on the back of the house along with a small porch.

This reminds me to tell everyone that it was not President Roosevelt who got us out of the Great Depression; it was World War II. War, my friend, is good business.

As the war continued, so did the old man's enhanced paychecks so he continued with additions to the house. He made the back porch into an small room which was occupied by my brother Freddie Lee. After adding Freddie's room, the old man converted part of the previously added back room into a bathroom.

Prior to the addition of the bathroom, we had a "two holer" out-house about twenty yards from the back door. Outhouses were one of the parts of the "good old days" that weren't so good. It was especially troublesome at night and during cold Missouri winters. During rainy spells, there was a lake of mud immediately behind the house on the way to the outhouse and we had to put down planks to get to the out-house.

The "building of the bathroom" will forever be etched into my memory because of the turmoil it created within our little familial microcosm. We were nowhere near the city sewer system so the only option available was to install a septic system. This is no simple nor easy task. It requires difficult, hard work, and a lot of backbreaking labor.

Since Freddie was the oldest of the three boys in the household, and a teenager, he was automatically elected to help the old man build the septic system.

When time permitted, both of them worked on it and it took weeks to complete the hole for the septic tank, the ditch for the drainage, and the hole for the distribution box. During the entire project, Freddie never shut up, never stopped complaining.

The second he picked up the shovel, he started whining. When he laid down the shovel, he continued to moan and bellyache about it. Even after it was finished, he would give a running commentary of the whole sordid affair, re-living each and every shovel full of dirt. He whined about how he was being used. It wasn't fair, it wasn't right, it wasn't his responsibility, he was being treated like a slave, he shouldn't have to work like this, and on and on and on.

He complained. He whined. He bellyached. He griped about it for the rest of his life.

The "Septic Tank Affair" was just one of the many "problems" between him and the old man. Freddie grew to hate him so much he ran away from home when he was seventeen and moved in with his girlfriend's family.

Freddie never let go of anything that happened between him and the old man. I think it became part of his reason for living. Even when he was in his seventies, before his death, I remember him complaining about the "Septic Tank Affair" and how ill-used he was, how the old man forced him to work as slave labor, how mean the old man was, and how he still hated him.

Frankly, it wasn't just the old man Freddie hated. He hated Harold and me, too. He had been the only child for so long he resented us and our "intrusion" on his life. He claimed that the old man used to beat him regularly just for fun, but I have no memory of such violent things. Sure, the old man used to give us a good smack every now and then, or he would give us some whacks with his belt from time to time, but there was no such thing as a regularly scheduled beating roster. Other than that, the old man just ignored us. He never had time for us and rarely acknowledged our existence.

Anyway, additions to the house continued. The last building project I remember was when the old man tore down the ramshackle mess of lumber he called the garage. He had built it before the war with junk wood taken from an old house that he helped tear down.

I guess somewhere in this little story I should mention that I would have had a sister but she died during birth. Her name was Delores Ray and she would have been the oldest of the kids had she lived, and the only girl. Two years later, Freddie Lee was born, ten years after Freddie was Herman Harold, Jr., and two years after Harold I made my entrance.

Naming me seemed to cause a modicum of friction among our household inhabitants.

The old man was working one of his double shifts while I was being born. Since he wasn't there, Mama was free to name me without his interference. I don't know where the "Michael" came from, but she named me "Charles" after her brother. The problem with that is that the old man absolutely hated her brother. Despised him. He disliked his brother-in-law so much he refused to call me by that name. And that, ladies and gentlemen, is why I've been called Michael all my life.

As the last one born, I sometimes wonder if my birth had anything to do with the eventual renal failure that killed Mama. We'll never know.

But, let's get back to the house and some of the things I remember before I forget them.

By the time the house was pretty well finished, it was laid out in a big square. Walking up to the front porch, the door opened into a front room with another room on the left. The kitchen was visible straight ahead and another room was off to the left of the kitchen. Behind the second room on the left was the bathroom that had caused so much turmoil in our home. To the right of the bathroom was Freddie's room, which had originally been a back porch.

Walking into the front room, there was a telephone on the wall near the front door. It was old and out-dated even when I was a child. I always heard it referred to as the "Kellogg Phone" because it was manufactured by the Kellogg Switchboard & Supply

Company. They were a major supplier of "bakelite" telephone exchange equipment.

It had a receiver on the left side, resting in a hook and a wire going to the main wooden box. It didn't even have a dial. You'd pick up the receiver, crank the handle on the right side of the phone, and speak into the mouthpiece on the front. The only person I ever remember calling was Grandma. When the operator said, "Number, please," I'd say, "288-R" and a few seconds later I could hear the phone ringing on the other end. Technology has advanced somewhat since then.

Keep walking after entering the front door, through that room, and there's the kitchen, with cabinets and a long counter on the right side of the room. The sink was there, too. To the left side of the room, was the icebox, not a refrigerator. A couple of times a week, a guy would deliver a large hunk of ice which would keep things in the icebox cool. At the back of the kitchen, on the left, was an ancient gas stove. A large box of wooden matches was kept in a dispenser on the wall to light the burners.

One thing I remember about the icebox was the glass milk bottles delivered by the milk man. The bottles had a large "bulb" at the top of the neck where cream gathered. We had a special small scoop for retrieving the cream and when there was enough, it could be whipped with a bit of salt to make butter.

Because butter was expensive, we mostly used oleomargarine. It came in "plastic" packets with a bubble of yellow food coloring which you would pop and mix with the margarine to make fake "yellow" butter. At the time, the law required that it be manufactured like this so unscrupulous merchants wouldn't try to pass off oleomargarine as real butter.

In the middle of the kitchen was a Formica table and chairs with vinyl seats and backs. It seems that there were always tears and rips in the vinyl that was repaired with old fabric "electrical" tape. I saw a set like it the other day in front of an antique dealer's shop. I hear they're worth a lot of money now. Back then it was the cheap way to go.

Leaving the kitchen through the door on the left brought you into the bedroom I had to share with Harold. Next to the bed was a large gas heater with Eisenglass windows. This heater was used to warm the entire house since we had no central heating and most of the time it was almost unbearably hot when we were trying to sleep. It was almost funny that here we were in the dead of winter, with freezing temperatures outside, and snow on the ground, yet Harold and I couldn't even lay under a sheet because it was so hot. When everyone else went to sleep, I would take off my pajamas and underwear and lay there naked.

It was around this time I remember having my first pet. Late one night, laying there in the sweltering room, I noticed something moving in the corner. When it came out into enough light for the to see what it was, it was a big rat. I watched him and tried to get him to come to me but he scurried away. Giving this some thought, I came up with a plan. The next night, I had sneaked a piece of bread and a small piece of cheese to bed. When the rat came out, I coaxed him over to the bed and gave him the bread and cheese. It only took a couple of nights for him to learn that I was his friend and had no intention of hurting him. He began to come to me and I would feed him and play with him. He was far from the evil and vicious animal that rats are supposed to be. He was just a cute little guy who was hungry. He never attacked me, bit me, or did anything hurtful toward me. He was my little friend.

It was unfortunate that being so young, I was also so naïve. I told Harold about it and told him not to say anything to anyone. Of course the next day the old man went out and bought a huge rat trap, the kind that can take off a finger if you're not careful. I never saw my little buddy again. And I never told Harold anything again, ever. If I learned one thing from this little episode, it was that if you want to keep a secret, you can't tell anyone . . . and I mean anyone.

Once the house had been upgraded with extra rooms and bath facilities, the old man decided to put a "car port" on the side of the house.

With the completion of the car port, the garage was torn down and the wood was used to augment the pig pen down the hill, behind the house, on the furthest edge of our property. These days, this would be called "re-purposing." Back then it was "making do with what the hell you got." As Grandma used to say, "Use it up, wear it out. Make it do, or do without."

The old man raised and sold hogs up to the time that Mama died. Next to the pig pen, we also had a garden that supplied tomatoes, potatoes, and corn. It was never enough to can, we just ate it as it grew.

The yard was fenced in with chicken-wire nailed to wooden posts and slats driven into the ground. A far cry from he spiffy vinyl fencing available today.

Some years ago, I visited Flat River (now called Park Hills) for my 40th High School Reunion and I stopped by the old place. I'm amazed it's still there. It's been cleaned up quite a bit, siding had been added, it was painted, the yard had been fixed up, and all-in-all it looked pretty good, better than when I lived there.

Looking back on all this, decades later, I think the place must have looked like something out of an Erskin Caldwell book; perhaps *God's Little Acre* or *Tobacco Road*.

No matter what it looked like, though, it was livable and I'm sure it must have looked pretty nice to someone who had no home. I mention this as a thought crosses my mind about Mama.

Every Christmas Mama would make up a little pallet-bed in a corner of our living room for the little girl or boy she would bring home from the orphanage in the nearby town of Farmington. She would pick up the little kid the day before Christmas and they would stay with us until the day after Christmas. That way, they had the whole day of Christmas to spend with a family, along with a nice Christmas dinner and some presents from Santa Claus. Mama made sure they returned to the orphanage with new clothes and toys. I don't remember a lot about Mama, but I do know she was a very special person, better than I'll ever be.

All things considered, I suppose it was a normal house in a normal neighborhood and we were a normal family for the 1940s.

Even by the furthest stretch of the imagination, it was nothing special . . . but it was home.

The old Kellogg Crank Telephone;
Just like the one in our front room.

22

Something's Wrong With Him

I have no idea if this story is true. Its veracity depends solely on the reliability of my Grandma and I wasn't told about it until I was barely into my teens. I have no memory of the event. Frankly, it embarrasses me to even tell it.

Our whole family was having Easter dinner at Grandma's house and since everyone was there it was a perfect setting for my Grandma to embarrass me. After all, that's one of the main purposes of family get-togethers. All of my aunts, uncles, and cousins were present and, just like any loving family, they enjoyed harassing and embarrassing me.

I have no idea how it came up, but Grandma mentioned to Aunt Teresa that I was unable to speak until I was well past three years of age. Here's what we were told at the dinner table:

Mama had, for some time, tried to get me to talk, to name things, to communicate with words in some manner. But it was all to no avail.

She became so worried over the "problem" she finally took me to Doc Jones. Everybody went to Doc Jones. He was the "company doctor" for the St. Joe Lead

Company.

We spent some time in his office, Mama explained the complexity of the problem, my eyes were tested, my hearing was tested, my reflexes were tested, just about everything I had was tested in some way or another. Doc was unable to find a single physical problem with me. When he unexpectedly jabbed me with a needle I yelped, but used no other linguistic verbiage.

After the examination, Doc shook his head, looked at me, and told Mama he had no idea what was wrong with me.

After sitting and considering things for a few minutes, he asked Mama, "How does he let you know if he wants or needs anything?"

Mama said, "He points at what he wants and grunts. If he can reach it, he gets it himself."

Doc got a quizzical look on his face and asked, "You mean to tell me that if he wants some milk or a piece of bread, he points at it, he grunts, and you give it to him?"

Mama nodded, indicating the affirmative, and said, "Yes."

Doc smiled, looked at me, shook his head, and told her, "Here's what I want you to do. Take him home and don't feed him anything until tomorrow. Don't give him any breakfast in the morning, either. When it's time for lunch, make him a sandwich and pour a glass of milk for him but don't give it to him. Put the sandwich and the milk on the table, point at the milk and say, 'Milk.' Point at the sandwich and say, 'Sandwich.' Do not, under

24

any circumstances, give him anything until he says milk or sandwich."

The next day, Mama did precisely as she had been instructed. Apparently it took less than a minute for me to say, "Milk," and "Sandwich."

From that moment on, I was never given anything until I specifically requested it by name.

After I did start talking, though, I think they were all sorry for what they did. Sometimes I wouldn't shut up.

At least that's the way the story was told to us at the dinner table.

It was either cold this day or Harold
and I were doing our impression of
Ming the Merciless.

The Boy With Green Teeth

I think it was around 1950 that I remember seeing a movie called *The Boy With Green Hair*. Such an idea doesn't raise an eyebrow now, but back then it was considered exceptionally peculiar.

The movie starred Dean Stockwell as the boy and Pat O'Brian as his Grampa. The storyline was that the boy's parents were in Europe just after the end of World War II and they had been killed while trying to help war orphans. The reason for the boy's hair turning green over-night was so he could become the spokesman for the idea that, "War is never the answer."

It was one of the first anti-war films I remember seeing. It was also one of the first movies demonstrating the liberal, post-war direction the "New Hollywood" was taking.

I never knew anyone with green hair when I was a kid, but I did know a kid who lived down the road from us who had green teeth. No kidding! His teeth were green! I'm pretty sure he never brushed his teeth in his life, at least at the time I knew him.

If green teeth weren't bad enough, he never seemed to get near a bathtub, either. His hair was so dirty that, even though combed, it always looked like a large clump of grease on his head. He was a strange little guy and as I think back on it, he must have had a hard life.

I don't think I ever saw him in anything new, especially his shoes. He walked with a sort of sliding-shuffle because he always wore shoes handed down from his father. Yes, I said his father, not an older brother. He also wore a belt about three times larger than he was. He told me one day it was his Dad's belt and he had to be careful with it. He wasn't allowed to punch a hole in it so it would fit him so he wrapped it around and through the belt loops on his overly large pants. His pants were so large he had to roll up the legs and there was always a large clump of fabric at the end of his skinny legs.

His father was known to be a chronically out of work drunkard who made money by "finding" things and selling them from the trunk of his beat up old Ford Model-A.

The front yard of his rented house was perpetually covered with empty, rusting beer cans; Stag, Falstaff, Budweiser, Pabst Blue-Ribbon, Miller High-Life, Schlitz, Carling Black Label, and anything else he could find to drink.

I'm talking about real beer cans here, not the flimsy, effeminate, aluminum recycle cans used today. And it was real beer, by Godfrey, not the pansy light beer sold today. It was real beer in real, steel beer cans with screw tops or flat tops requiring a "church key" to open.

His father also well know in the

neighborhood for his propensity toward foul language. He was so skilled in its use, it bordered on eloquence. He could have turned professional if such a career existed. I heard him once as he "explained" something to his son just seconds before slapping the snot out of him.

He had a talent for cursing that was almost mesmerizing. He would split his profane invectives and insert other curse words in the middle of them.

I could easily offer further detailed examples of his verbiage, but it is not my intention to sensationalize such vulgarisms.

This habit of colloquial cursing affected his son to such a degree that he "almost" swore at all times without actually doing so.

The peculiar thing is that if the kid's father ever heard him use profanity, he would give the kid a resounding slap on the side of the head with the admonition to, "Watch yer god-damned mouth, ya little bastard."

Before giving an example of this "almost swearing" I must first explain that we had one of the first television sets on our block. It was an old beat up, Admiral Television Set with a seven inch screen, but it worked. It will come as no surprise when I say that the kid's family did not own a television. I doubt they even owned a radio.

On occasion, the boy with green teeth would ask if he could come into our house and watch television, but he couldn't say television. He had a slight speech impediment in addition to having trouble putting together a coherent sentence. He would mix regular words with half-way swear words and end up with his own vocabulary. His term for television was *sun-a-bizion.*

One day, while I was sitting in the yard, he slide-shuffled up to me and said, "I wanna watch yer *sun-a-bizzion!*" I politely informed him that I was very busy reading my *Human Torch* comic book. He became very upset and said, "Lemme in yer Gof-Ram house! I wanna see *sun-a-bizion!*" I told him to leave me alone and to go home.

He shuffle-stomped out of the yard and into the middle of the road, turned around and yelled at me, *"Gof-Ram-Summa-Bazzars."* He picked up a rock and threw it at me, just missing my head. I got up from the tree I was sitting against and made a run for him. He grabbed his too-large belt and his too-large pants and began to slide-shuffle-run down the road. I picked up a rock and threw it at him.

Now, here's the extraordinary thing that happened. I honestly didn't mean to hit him with the rock. I just meant to let him know that if he threw a rock at me, I'd throw one back at him. I threw the rock off to the left of him so it would miss him. Unfortunately, he veered to the left and both he and the rock ended up at the same place at the same time. Now as we all know from our physics class, two objects cannot occupy the same space at the same time. The rock caught him in the back of the head and opened a gash about an inch long. As with most injuries to the head, it began to bleed quite a bit.

Mama heard him screaming and crying. She came out of the house, brought him into the yard, and told him to sit there for a minute. She also asked him to please be quiet.

She went in the house and a few moments later came out with a wash rag. She cleaned his wound and put a band-aid on it. She gave him a hug and said, "You'd better go home now."

All this time he leered at me with hate in his little eyes. I began to feel sorry for him. As he started to leave the yard he looked back at me and said, "*Summa-Bazzar.*"

When he was well on his way down the road, Mama took me onto our front porch and told me she understood why I did what I did, but that I should never have thrown that rock. She said he had enough problems and he didn't need people throwing rocks at him, too.

As she walked through the front door, she turned back to me and said, "If he comes back and wants to watch television, tell him it's broken and we don't know when it'll be working again. Then just come inside."

Mama was a nicer person than I'll ever be.

In our front yard around 1950.
The little girl on the left is my
cousin, Charlene Criteser. I
don't remember the little
girl in the middle.

The Boomerang

Even when Mama was alive, my old man pretty much ignored my brothers and me. It may well be that this rare acknowledgment is the reason I remember this story.

We weren't the richest family in Flat River, nor were we destitute. I think the old man probably brought home about twenty-five dollars a week from the mines and back then it was a decent amount of money. Unless it was absolutely necessary, he never spent anything on us kids, but one time he did and I remember it well. It's one of those good news and bad news stories.

For some curious reason, he came home early one day with presents for both Harold and me. I don't remember what he gave Harold, but I got a cheap plastic boomerang glued onto a thin piece of cardboard. I think it cost a nickel.

I read the instructions on the back of the cardboard two or three times to make sure I understood how to make it work.

When I felt confident about the intricacies of this ingenious Aboriginal device, I took the boomerang out to our back yard.

I held it according to the instructions, angled it slightly to get some lift, and threw it with everything I had. Boy, did that thing sail into the air. It went up and up and out and out, further and further. It went all the way out of the backyard, over the garden, over the pig-pen, and down into the jungle beyond.

As I stood there, watching it descend and disappear into the tree and bramble filled jungle, I began to suspect that something was amiss. I stood there for a few moments, giving this problem due consideration. The boomerang never returned.

I was certain the instructions said it was supposed to make a big circle and come back to me, but I was apparently, blatantly wrong. It never made the slightest attempt at any kind of circle. It just went straight down into that treacherous "no man's land" behind our house. I wondered if the company made a mistake and put a "one-way-arang" on the cardboard. I don't know.

I continued to contemplate this conundrum. I read the instructions again. It sure seemed to me that I did everything as directed.

Now, I knew I had been told to never go down into the wasteland beyond our property, but I was sure that this was a unique case and it warranted a search of the area. After all, this thing cost the old man a whole nickel.

I carefully made my way through the briars and thorns, hanging onto the trees as best I could. I was doing just fine until I stepped on one rock that gave way, slipping into the huge hole in the ground. I almost went with it.

Considering it today, I'm sure the hole

wasn't as big as I thought it was, but when you're less than three feet tall, any kind of hole can seem extraordinarily large and deep.

I kept my grip on the tree (which was really a very large bush) and was able to climb back to stable ground. Making my way back up the steep incline proved to be a much more daunting task that the trek down. When I finally made it back to our yard, I noticed that I was bleeding all over. I had quite a few bruised and numerous cuts from the thorns I had encountered. My shoes were also a mess.

I must have wasted about an hour down there, in the belly of the beast, and all to no avail. I never found that stupid boomerang. And what did I get for all my trouble? I got tired, sweaty, cut, bruised, and angry.

Walking into the kitchen, I saw the old man sitting at the table reading a newspaper. As I walked past him I said, "Thanks for the swell toy." He never looked at me. He just said, "Yeah."

When Mama saw me, she was upset. She took me into the bathroom and began to clean me up. She said, "You're not supposed to go down to the sinkhole. If something happened to you, what would I do without my Mikey?"

That hurt worse than losing a boomerang and almost falling into the sinkhole. I never went near the place again.

The Spelling Bee Incident

Before I tell this story, I must make it perfectly clear that this event occurred at a time when television was a new technological advance and most people still listened to radio shows. One of the radio shows Mama listened to was sponsored by a product named "Duz" detergent.

The product's slogan at the time was, "Duz does everything," meaning it could be used to wash dishes, do the laundry, clean tubs and toilets, and just about anything else. The manufacturers of Duz made it sound like a bona fide miracle product. It was also a product that came with a surprise in every box! Goblets, dinner plates, flatware, dish towels, teacups, coffee cups, saucers, and everything else a home could not be without. If I remember correctly, the glassware was a sultry, smoky grey that would match any décor.

Theoretically, it was possible to accumulate a full set of house-wares simply by faithfully purchasing a box of Duz every week. There was even a network of housewives keeping track of who had what and they all traded duplicates to complete their collections.

Now, on with the story.

School is a place where people are supposed to receive an education. Sometimes, however, the educational process includes subject matter which is thoroughly unintentional and is far from the school's planned curriculum. Such was the case with me.

When I was in the second grade I received one my earliest lessons in the odious nature of adults, learning just how mean, petty, and unfair they can be to small children. It was a harsh lesson for someone of my naïve and trusting nature and I shall never forget it.

As a child, with my Penny Pencil in my hand and my Big Chief Tablet on a table, I would put pencil to paper and jot down stories that popped into my little head. I could read and write before I went to school.

As an adult, I've penned a number of books, including biographies, military histories, play-scripts, and computer manuals. During my employment with the Union-Tribune newspaper in San Diego, California, one of my friends there went as far as to use the term "wordsmith" when referring to my acumen and abilities.

I seem, however, to be getting off the track here, so I need to get back to what I call "The Spelling Bee Incident."

As I've said, I was in the second grade when this happened, which would make me about six or seven years old. There was a big spelling bee in the school that year and I was one of the finalists in the competition. The winner was to receive some sort of really swell prize, even though I don't remember what it was.

The rules of the Spelling Bee were simple. The student was given a word to spell and after spelling it correctly, the word had to be used in a sentence to make sure the student understood its meaning and proper usage.

We went round after round until there were two of us left; me and a little girl.

In addition to being a good speller, I was well known throughout the school as the "class entertainer." I had a certain flair for the dramatic.

You can imagine my surprise when the teacher reached into the fishbowl containing the words to be spelled and came out with a piece of paper with the word "does" on it. She said, "Now, spell the word 'does' and use it in a sentence."

I couldn't help myself when this incredibly amazing opportunity presented itself. Here was a chance to spell the word, win a prize, and make a hit with the audience all in one easy step.

I slowly and carefully said, "D-O-E-S. Does. Duz does everything!" I smiled and waited for the reaction from the other students, which was forthcoming in the form of laughs and chuckles.

I was both "flabbered" and "gasted" at the same time when the teacher said, "That's wrong. You're disqualified. You can't use a proper name in a sentence like that." She then proclaimed my competitor, the little girl, to be the winner and handed her the prize.

I complained, saying, "You can't do that. It's not fair."

The teacher gave me a dirty look and said, "I'm the teacher. You're the student. I make the rules and you follow them. Sit down and be quiet."

I looked at the other students, expecting someone, anyone to say something in my defense. Where was the anger? Where was the outrage at this grievous injustice? But, no one seemed to care. They appeared to be enjoying this little drama.

Infuriated by this, I said, "You old snot rag!"

The teacher retaliated by sending me to the principal's office where I was threatened with a sound whipping if I didn't, " . . . stop this nonsense and show respect for the teacher." I was told to go back to class and apologize for my impertinence. Instead, I walked out of the principal's office, down the stairs, out the door, and I went straight home. I could not have been more disgusted.

When I got home I told my sad tale of woe to Mama. She patted me on the head and said, "It's not worth the trouble. I think you should stay home tomorrow and take a day off from school."

I stayed home the next day and I remember Mama saying she had to go out for a little while. I was to stay inside and wait until she got back. When she returned about an hour later, she made me a sugar sandwich and told me to sit at the kitchen table. I remember hearing her on the phone, saying something about, " . . . giving them a piece of my mind."

It was discovered later that the teacher and the little girl's mother were friends but by that time, the whole incident had blown over. It was yesterday's news.

When I returned to class, things were different. The other students stayed away from me and the teacher simply ignored me. For the rest of the year, I was never asked questions, I was given written assignments to do at home, and I was left to my own devices, which suited me just fine.

I often wonder if Mama had anything to do with that.

Royal duties are multitude: Noblesse oblige.
I'm in the "float" next to Linda Rasche.
Harold is next to the tall kid and between
Linda and Harold is her brother, David.
I don't remember the others.

King For A Day

In the summer of 1950 Flat River held a *Tiny Tot King and Queen Competition.*

The idea behind the festivities was to crown a Tiny Tot King and Queen while promoting business in downtown Flat River. To be truthful, I don't remember much about what happened, but I was told about it later.

When I was a teenager, living with my grandparents, my Grandma told me that about two dozen little boys and girls were entered into the contest and I was one of them.

The voting procedure was simple. When a purchase was made at any of the participating stores, a ballot was given to the customer with the amount of the purchase written on the ballot. There was one vote for every penny spent. The ballot was then completed by the customer. They would enter the name of one boy and one girl and the ballot was then placed in a collection box in the store.

Everything seemed to be fair and impartial until Mama overheard some women talking in our *Scott's Five and Dime Store.*

One of the women was the mother of a little boy in the race for Tiny Tot King and she was bragging to the other women about how she had everything fixed. She said the election was in the bag because she had started a campaign to have her son win the crown. She had conspired with her neighbors and they were building a network of people to come downtown, buy things, and vote for her child.

Mama thought this was not only unfair, but shameful. It was her opinion that the competition should be based on normal, everyday purchases. People shouldn't be buying things they didn't need just to get an unfair voting advantage. When she discovered this concentrated effort for voter fraud, she was very upset.

She discussed the situation with Grandma and Grandma agreed with her. It displeased both of them to know that something that was supposed to fun and simple was being corrupted. They both agreed that it was tantamount to cheating for people to purchase things they didn't normally buy or need. Teaming up, they went into action.

Mama contacted all of the people she knew at the Esther Baptist Church and explained the situation. Not only did the church members begin to purchase items, the church officials began visit downtown Flat River businesses to purchase things needed at the church.

Grandma responded as well. Being a member of a number of associations, lodges, and clubs, she contacted all of her friends in those organizations and explained what was happening. They, in turn, began to visit downtown Flat River businesses for their consumer needs and they asked their friends to do so, too.

The one stipulation made clear by Mama and Grandma was that people were to purchase only those things they would normally buy, nothing more. Neither woman wanted to be part of the voter fraud business.

As things progressed, it became abundantly clear that it was a mistake to offend Mama and Grandma. They were two very clever and resourceful women. They had a lot of connections.

The end result was that I was elected to the throne as Tiny Tot King. It was a landslide of proportions only dreamed of by anyone with political aspirations.

I was, indeed, king for a day, Tiny Tot King, that is.

TINY TOT KING AND QUEEN

What can I say?
Humility forbids further comment.

Polio

Very few people in this country remember polio and its devastating effects. The full name for the disease is poliomyelitis and I remember how horrible it was.

In 1952 Polio was looked upon as a plague and children were often kept at home so they would not come in contact with other children who might have the virus. Kids were kept away from swimming pools, lakes, and rivers because it was thought that water might contain the virus.

Even in the late 1800s, polio was a horrific problem and it continued into the 20th century, increasingly destroy lives until Jonas Salk created the first vaccine in 1952.

It was polio that paralyzed Franklin D. Roosevelt in 1921, causing him to use leg braces for the rest of his life.

As I play the memory through my mind, I can see the long line of children at Emerson Elementary School waiting for their vaccinations. Mothers brought in pre-school age children and babies for vaccinations.

There were a number of doctors and nurses on hand to give the shots. A corner of the basement had been set up with sterilization equipment for the hypodermic syringes. Disposable, plastic syringes and tiny needles had not been devised yet. The medical profession still used glass syringes and large, painful needles. After each use, the syringes and needles were sterilized and reused.

Salk's vaccine, made from inactivated (dead) polio-virus, was first tested in 1952. A later "oral" vaccine, developed by Albert Sabin, was given by putting a drop of the vaccine on a sugar cube.

The symptoms of the disease were simple enough. A person would feel tired and achy, often running a mild fever. They would go to bed, feeling like they were getting a cold, and wake up the next morning paralyzed. It was that quick and nasty.

In severe cases, children would be paralyzed for life, requiring heavy steel braces to walk. Extreme cases would often require the use of an "iron lung."

The iron lung was developed in the late 1920s to assist people so paralyzed they were unable to breathe on their own. It was a huge, fully-pressurized tank in which the person lived because their bodies were unable to perform the normal "breathing process." The tank's pressure was increased and decreased rhythmically to induce artificial respiration.

I knew a kid from Desloge who had polio. It caused so much damage to his muscles, he was relegated to spending most of his life in an iron lung. Ironically, he was considered to be one of the "lucky" ones, being able to get out of the machine for a couple of hours every day.

When he was independent of his

mechanical respirator, he used his time to optimum advantage. He had a small business engraving I.D. bracelets and dog-tags, which were popular at the time. For a dollar, he would engrave whatever you wanted on the item you bought from him. Some folks brought special items to him for engraving. Although he charged a dollar for the service, everyone I knew gave him five to ten dollars as a "tip." That was a lot of money back then.

During the 1950s, most businesses had "March of Dimes" donation cards on their counters with small slots for dimes to be inserted. It was only dimes, but they collected a lot of them. I remember seeing a picture of Elvis Presley with a March of Dimes sign behind him talking to a little girl who appeared to be about five years old. She was wearing braces and using crutches.

The kid from Desloge died in 1954.

An Iron Lung used during the Polio
epidemic of the 1940s and 1950s.

Jesse James

I've never been a good traveler. If I'm not driving a car, I have to be in the passenger seat. If it weren't for Dramamine, I'd never, ever get on an airplane or a boat, especially a boat.

It was especially bad during my three years in the army. On the way to my permanent duty station in Germany, I flew over the Atlantic ocean in a "jet-assisted" propeller driven airplane, landing in Frankfort, Germany after a twenty hour trip.

As horrible as that was, it was nothing compared to the nine days I spent coming home aboard a troop transport ship with almost two thousand other soldiers. On the plus side, the ship was returning to the states and I was mustering out of the army. Our "bunks" were stacked six high and I was on the bottom. I would lay on the floor, roll over, and in bed. Not only were there times I thought I was going to die, there were more times when I hoped that I would, just to put me out of my misery. It was an unspeakably hideous trip.

The worst case of motion-sickness I've suffered, however, was purposely induced by a doctor who was supposed to find out why I get so sick. It was a complete failure and waste of time. After enduring her ghastly torture, the doctor had no answers.

She put little tubes into my ears that spurted jets of warm and cold water on my eardrums. A couple of minutes was all I could stand of that. Almost falling out of the chair, I crawled to the waiting room where I laid on the floor until I could halfway stand up. My wife drove home because I was physically unable to raise my head to look out the window. Arriving at home, I crawled into bed and went to sleep. The only cure I've ever found for these horrible episodes is to sleep it off. It hasn't changed for decades and I doubt it ever will.

Even as a small child, I suffered from excruciating instances of this disorder. On family outings, even on a short trip, if I was in the backseat, I would become appallingly ill. No matter where we went, Mama would never leave the house unless she had an ample supply of paper bags in the car. In most cases, she'd keep me on her lap unless it was a very long trip. On those occasions, I would lay on the floor behind the front seat and try to sleep through it all.

People who have never experienced and suffered from this problem are utterly incapable of understanding how terrible it is. There was one time, especially, when one of my puking disasters occurred because someone thought I was "making it up."

When I was about five, Harold was in the Cub Scouts. I was allowed to attend meetings and outings as their "mascot."

Speaking of mascots, I was the "Keebler Elf" once, but that's another story.

Our little scout troop had accumulated some money by scouring the town for soda bottles and redeeming them at the local Royal Crown Cola plant. In those days, a dollar was worth a dollar. We ended up with enough money to pay for a Saturday outing to Merrimac Caverns and we were all looking forward to it (well, maybe not me so much).

The big day finally arrived and all the scouts (and their mascot) were assembled at the elementary school for the trip. We boarded a beat-up, old, yellow bus that looked like it was on its last legs.

There was a "lady in charge" who was telling everyone what to do and how to do it. When it came time to load me onto the bus, Mama took the lady aside, handed her some paper bags, and painstakingly explained to her that she had to put me in the front seat. She warned the woman about what would happen if I were put anywhere other than in the front. Mama didn't say what "might" happen, she made it crystal clear that it "would" happen if I wasn't in the front seat.

Per instructions, I was put in the front seat right behind the driver and we began our journey. So far, so good.

Arriving at Merrimac Caverns, we were escorted to the entrance where the lady in charge paid for our tickets and we spent an hour or so touring the caverns. Surprisingly, I was having fun.

Before getting back on the bus, we were

given sack lunches and we ate at some picnic tables in the area.

We got back on the bus for the trip home. I was doing fine so far, no problems at all.

Then, for some unexplained reason, the bus driver left the main road. Hmmm, I thought, this isn't the way home. We twisted and turned up a hill to a dilapidated, little cabin on the side of the road. I was no longer having fun.

When the bus stopped, we were all wondering where we were and what we were doing there. The lady in charge herded us off the bus, lined us up, and said, "Well, kids, I've got a real treat for you. I know it wasn't planned, but I decided that since we were close by, we should stop in here so you could all meet," ..... wait for it ..... "Jesse James!"

Holey Moley! We all looked at each other and couldn't believe our ears. Jesse James! The famous murdering, thieving, robber outlaw. I was pretty sure I had seen him get killed at a Saturday Matinee, but, then, I was just a kid, what did I know.

She had us walk single file through the small door of the small cabin where we were told to stand in two lines against a wall. Then some really old woman wheeled out a really, really old guy in a wheel chair.

"Kids," said the lady in charge, "Meet Jesse James."

As we stood there looking at this ancient, frail human being, I thought to myself, "He doesn't look like a dangerous criminal. He's not even carrying a gun."

Then one of the older kids said, "I thought Bob Ford shot you in the back."

The old man just made a sort of chuckling sound and the woman behind him said, "Thet was jist a made up sorta story. Pappy here had ever' thing fixed up so's ever' body'd think he wuz dead. Then he could start a-fresh, with nobody chasin' him or nuthin'"

I was much too young to comprehend all this, but others were much more skeptical. One of the older kids had read a book that said Jesse James was born in 1847 and since this trip happened around 1949, that would have made him over a hundred years old. The kid asked the old woman about it and she said, "Yep, he be a hunerd an' two."

The kid wasn't buying any of this hogwash. "Well," he said, "Then why did Bob Ford go along with this whole thing when he knew he'd be called a coward for shooting him in the back? Nobody likes a back-shooter."

The old lady responded by wheeling the old man around and out of the room, mumbling to herself. When she slammed the door we all looked a the lady in charge. Finally she said, "I guess we better get going now."

Boy, that was a bust.

As we were getting back on the broken down bus, for some inexplicable reason, the lady in charge decided that I had been doing so well I didn't need to ride in the front the rest of the way home. She sat in the front seat with another one of the kids and she put me in the very back of the bus. I protested to no avail. She said I'd be fine, that I should quit "play acting," and I should stop all this nonsense.

We were on the road for about fifteen minutes when I puked the first time, all over the floor, with a little splatter on the kid next to me. That made him sick, too. Things began to deteriorate.

The lady in charge didn't bother to stop the bus. She grabbed me by the hand, dragged me to the front of the bus and, sat me in the front seat again. But, by this time, the damage was done. There was no turning back. Once the evil Genie was out of the bottle, all bets were off.

I puked on the floor next to the driver and the stink began to permeate the bus. Windows were opened, kids got as far away from me as possible, and I just laid in the seat like a slug. Then I progressed to the dry heaves. I was not enjoying this trip at all.

We finally made it back to the school parking lot and every body ran for the door and started jumping out even before the bus stopped.

I slowly stumbled out of the bus and just sat down on the gravel, holding my head.

Mama was there, waiting for us. She figured out pretty quickly what was going on. She walked over to the lady in charge and said, "What did I tell you? You put him in the back didn't you? This is all your fault. I hope you're happy."

With that she took my hand and slowly walked me to the car. I crawled inside, behind the front seat, and laid there. Harold, who had offered no help whatsoever during this debacle, climbed into the front seat.

Mama put a paper bag in my hand and said, "It'll be okay, Mikey. We'll be home in a couple of minutes."

No, it's not really Napoleon. It's only me.

Harold, Mama, and me, 1947. We're posing
in front of our tasteful, well-kept yard, and
our expensive, hand-crafted, designer fence.

Great-Great Aunt Mary

James Agee spent years working on his autobiographical novel *A Death in the Family*. Beginning it in 1948, he almost had it finished when he abruptly died of a heart attack in 1955. Luckily, for the reading public, the book was given final edits and published by McDowell-Oblensky in 1957. It won the Pulitzer Prize in 1958. The novel was adapted by Tad Mosel in 1961 into a play called *All the Way Home*. A Pulitzer was awarded to the play, too.

Material from both the book and the play was used to create a motion-picture called *All The Way Home* in 1963. Robert Preston and Jeanne Simmons starred in the film. To add reality, it was filmed in the Knoxville, Tennessee neighborhood where James Agee grew up.

A Death in the Family has been included in a list of the 100 best English-language novels written in the 20th Century.

Now I can continue with my story.

When I first read Mr. Agee's book, I was stunned. I wondered if he had been hiding outside our house, peeking in our windows, and writing about the Province family. The parallels of his childhood and my childhood were astonishing.

Our families, of course, were vastly different but, for the most part, the family dynamics and events in Mr. Agee's book closely resembled much that occurred in my early life and childhood.

One particularly striking similarity was the Follett family visit to "Granmaw Follett." Like the Folletts, the Province family once embarked on a comparable pilgrimage.

Grandpa Province had been told that his Aunt Mary was not doing well. She was the last one left from the generation of Grandpa's parents. Born in 1847, she had just turned one-hundred-and-three and she was "feelin' downright poorly." Grandpa felt the situation warranted a visit to cheer her up.

I had never even thought about Grandpa having aunts and uncles but when I did give it some consideration, I realized that his parents and his grand-parents were around during the Civil War and, further back, at the founding of our nation. Grandpa's grandpa, for instance, was born in the late 1700s. He was alive when the United States was having birthing pains. I think that's pretty darn interesting.

As I was saying before I interrupted myself, Aunt Mary was "feelin' downright poorly" so we piled into our 1948 Ford and took off. Because neither Grandpa nor Grandma ever learned to drive, they relied on their children and friends to provide them with transportation. When I was old enough, I drove them everywhere they needed to go.

So, here we were in the car on our way

to Aunt Mary's place. I, as usual, was lying on the floor behind the front seats because of my gruesome motion-sickness problem.

I had no idea where we were going or where we went. By the sounds, I knew we were mostly on gravel roads but the closer we got, the less it sounded like a road at all. It was more akin to a wagon trail through a forest. It was up, down, and round hills, driving slowly and carefully over gullies and creeks that could only be forded in dry weather. As she always did, Grandma made continual comments and gave a running summation of what everyone else was able to see. Grandma was a woman to be reckoned with. I had never experienced anything like this and I began to imagine myself riding in the back of a Conestoga wagon on the way to California.

Eventually, finally, we emerged from a grove of old growth hickory trees into a small meadow. In the middle of the clearing rested a very small house surrounded by what once must have been a picket fence. We bumped and bounced our way up to the gate, my old man turned off the engine, and the car wheezed to a stop.

We crawled out of the car. My old man, Mama, Grandpa, Grandma, Harold, and me. I remember it being extremely cold and Grandpa making the remark that, "Damn. It's colder than a witch's tit out here." I always thought Grandpa was pretty funny.

The house looked like it was built around the same time as Grandpa's farmhouse, the one he was born in near Irondale. To say the least, it was very old and not well kept. If it had ever been painted, there was no evidence left to prove it.

Grandpa carefully opened the rickety gate, let everyone through, and then put it back, wrapping the wire ring around one of the pickets to keep the gate from falling off. We trudged to the house where I could see smoke boiling out of the chimney.

An old woman, Aunt Mary's daughter, met us at the door. I think they called her Lucy. As we filed through the small framed door, one at a time, we entered an exceedingly small room. There was a window on the wall next to the door and another one on the wall to the left of us. Each window had been closed onto folded newspapers and newspapers had been stuffed into the cracks around the window. I would be willing to wager that when the house was built, newspapers were also stuffed between the walls during construction for insulation. They used what they had in "them there days."

An old, ratty couch sat under the window on the left. On the right was the oldest woman I had ever seen. She was sitting in a rocking chair next to a red-hot pot-bellied stove. Past the stove was another rocking chair. Both chairs had quilts covering them for padding and warmth. Directly across from the front door was another small door that went into the kitchen.

Immediately to the right was a set of very steep stairs going up and to the left. I thought it was peculiar that there was no railing on the side of the stairs. A box of split logs sat in front of the stove.

Lucy ordered everyone to, "Have yerselves a sit-down." That proved to be impossible since there was just enough room for Grandpa and Grandma on the couch. The rest of us stood there. Lucy "deliberated" on this situation for a few moments and said, "I reckon I'd best git some chairs outta the kitchen fer sittin' on."

She opened the door to the kitchen and a harsh blast of freezing air filled the room. She brought out two chairs, which is all that would fit in the cramped area. Harold sat on Grandma's lap and I sat on Mama's lap.

Then they started talking, or rather "palaverin' " as Lucy referred to it.

Actually, it was Grandpa, Grandma, and Lucy doing the palaverin'. I listened and tried to make sense of it all, but Lucy was hard to understand and they talked about people, places, and things I had never heard of, things completely alien to me.

They talked about being kids in the 1880s, who married who, who had kids, how many kids lived or died, who sold their farms, who moved to the city, whose kids went to college, and everything imaginable. I had no idea who they were talking about.

After an hour's worth of this, Lucy jumped up and said, "I got sumpthin' ta show ye." She went up the steep, rail-less staircase and when she opened the door to the second floor, another blast of frigid air enveloped the small front room. She returned with an old, beat up album of photographs and a box of tin-types. Holding the photographs at an angle, you could see the sheen of the silver nitrate on the paper. These pictures gave new meaning to the word old. I often wonder what happened to all those family heirlooms.

They went through all the photos and tin-types commenting on each and every one of them, recalling memories and stories about every person in each picture.

As I watched and listened to them I inspected the small room again. As my gaze fell on the kitchen door and the staircase, my young mind realized that during these freezing winter months they sequestered themselves into this little room and lived here throughout the winter. There was no electricity, no propane, no running water, and no indoor toilet. It was impossible to heat the entire house with this one little stove.

I began to concentrate on the 103-year-old woman who was my great-great aunt.

She sat in her rocking chair completely wrapped in a quilt, except for her head and hands. Her face and hands were wrinkled but it wasn't a kind of wrinkling I had ever seen before. Her skin seemed to have a sheen, like a piece of wrinkled silk. Her dark, paper-thin skin was mottled with almost black age spots and her lips were surrounded by skin that reminded me of a turtle's mouth. She had no teeth.

While her body may have been failing,

however, her mind seemed to be pretty sharp for someone over a hundred years old.

She was attentive to everything going on in the room and she listened to every word being said. She kept her eyes closed most of the time but opened them when something in particular interested her. I couldn't help being fascinated by her left eye; it was almost completely white.

Once in a while she would say something but it was more like a croak than words. Grandpa's stories about being a kid on the farm made her laugh.

I was somewhat startled the first time Aunt Mary reached down, picked up the coffee can next to her chair, and spit a huge glop of tobacco juice into it. I thought it was exceedingly funny. I had seen men do it, of course, but never a woman. Women weren't even supposed to smoke, let alone "chaw tabakky."

After what seemed to me like hours, the conversations began to dwindle and fell into a lull. The quietness of the place was amazing. No matter how long it is between visits, there's only so much that can be said. When it came time for us to leave, Grandpa made sure the wood box was full in front of the stove to save Aunt Mary from trudging out in the freezing weather. He even let me put a couple of logs in the box for them.

When we first entered the house, I was struck by the overwhelming odor in the room and it failed to improve throughout our visit. I noticed a large pee-pot in the corner covered with a heavy cloth. I wondered how often it got used and, more importantly, how often it got emptied. At first, I thought it peculiar that a small wash tub sat under Aunt Mary's rocking chair but after a while I figured out why it was there. As we were leaving, I admitted to myself that being able to stand up and walk to an outhouse, even in freezing weather, wasn't such a bad thing after all.

After all the goodbyes were said and we were back on the road, I could still smell the house in everyone's clothes. We dropped Grandma and Grandpa at their house and then went home. As we were walking into our living room, Mama said, "Everybody take off all your clothes right now. I'm doing a load of laundry."

The next time I saw Grandpa, I asked him about Aunt Mary's eye. He said she had an accident when she was a little girl and it had been like that most of her life.

Great great Aunt Mary died the next summer. She made it to one hundred and four by one week.

The Grand Theater in Desloge where
the KFMO Barn Dance was held.

The KFMO Barn Dance, held in the Desloge
Theater around 1948. There was talk that I
might be asked to perform here when I was
about five years old.

The Christmas Show At KFMO

I've heard of "Old Hollywood" actors who claimed to be "born in a trunk." They were children of families working in Vaudeville before radio and motion-pictures destroyed that form of entertainment. Judy Garland, Mickey Rooney, Baby LeRoy, and Jackie Cooper come to mind. I doubt that many people will recognize those names unless they're movie buffs who love old black and white films from the 1930s and 1940s.

Me? Born in a trunk? Not hardly. If anything, I was "born in a lead mine." My family (and most of my relatives} made a living either as miners or farmers. Show business was foreign to them, something that one of them maybe, possibly, perhaps had read about in a book once, if they ever read a book. The only connection between my folks and show business was to go to the movies, listen to radio, or watch television.

"So," you are probably saying right now, "What does this have to do with your little stories?"

I'm glad you asked. Here is my "Christmas Story."

The year was 1949. I was five years old. It was less than a week before Christmas.

Flat River's radio station, KFMO, had

been broadcasting for a little over two years. Their first broadcast was on August 8, 1947 in the dining room of the old National Hotel on Main Street. The station's permanent building was completed in 1948 and that's where Mama took me for the 1949 Christmas broadcast.

The concept was simple and to the point. Prior to the Christmas show, the station requested that interested mothers mail in a postcard with their names, addresses, and telephone numbers along with the names and ages of their children. They were asked to include a note as to why their child should be chosen for the show. Mama followed the instructions, told them I was five years old, and explained that I could sing.

1949 was the year Gene Autry recorded his most popular and famous song; *Rudolph The Red-Nosed Reindeer*. I had heard the song numerous times on the radio and had it memorized.

When the broadcast time approached, Mama and I were ushered into a small room with about a dozen other mothers and children.

One by one each mother and child was brought to the microphone sitting on a small table and the child was introduced to the audience. The announcer talked with each kid, asking them what they wanted for Christmas and why.

This was long before kids were taught by their liberal parents to always ask for "World Peace." Invariably they wanted regular "stuff" like Tinker Toys, Lincoln Logs, Mickey Mouse items, rocking horses, and little red wagons. Footballs were occasionally requested.

For some reason, Mama and I were the last ones brought to the microphone. Upon consideration, I think it was a setup.

The announcer talked with me for a little while, asked me what I wanted for Christmas, and that's when I got the first taste of laughter from an audience:

Announcer: "What do you want for Christmas this year, Mikey?"

Mikey: "I want a money making machine."

There was a two or three second delay from the audience and the announcer gave me a funny look. Then he and the audience started to laugh. That really cracked him up. He could hardly stop laughing. He said, "I think we all want a money making machine, don't we folks?"

It was one of those rare moments and it caught him just right. He kept laughing until the end of the show. Every time he looked at me, I just smiled, and he would start laughing again.

When things calmed down a little, he asked if I could sing *Rudolph The Red-Nosed Reindeer* for the radio audience. I said, "Yes, sir, I can," and I did.

Since there was no musical accompaniment, I even supplied musical sounds where instrumental interludes would have been. It is not my intention to brag, but I pretty well brought down the house. People even called the radio station asking me to sing another song.

After the show, the announcer talked with Mama and invited us back the next year. There was even talk of having me appear on KFMO's weekly *Barn Dance* which was broadcast from the Grand Theater in Desloge, a small town next to Flat River. The *Barn Dance* was Flat River's version of *The Grand Ol' Opry*.

But, none of that happened. As the old saying goes, "Life goes on."

By the time Christmas came around in 1950, Mama was showing visible signs of the disease that killed her. Things began to change drastically in my young life.

If she hadn't died, I would have sung every song in the world for her.

Saying Goodbye

Century-Fox produced a movie called, *Cheaper by the Dozen*. It was the story of Frank and Lillian Gilbreth and their ten children. A sequel came out in 1952 called *Belles on Their Toes*. It dealt with the family problems after the death of Frank Gilbreth.

Watching a DVD of the sequel recently, I was struck by one particular scene showing the Gilbreth children sneaking into a hospital to see their mother. They were running past a large sign that read, "No Children Under The Age Of Twelve Are Allowed During Visiting Hours."

Similar regulations were in place at the Bethesda Hospital in Saint Louis, Missouri where Mama died of "anuria." The anuria was caused by "Glomerulonephritis," a disease that injures the "blood filtering" part of the kidney. The "acute" form of the disease develops suddenly. The chronic form may develop without symptoms over several years. Both lead to complete kidney failure. This is what killed Mama on the 27th of February, 1952. She was forty years old. I was seven.

Bethesda, like other hospitals at the time, adhered to the strict principle that children were not allowed as visitors.

The last couple of weeks during Mama's

illness she was bed-ridden and unable to travel. It was decided that she would be kept as comfortable as possible and she would be allowed to die in the hospital.

Patients at Bethesda were both nursed and ministered to by Catholic Nuns. One of the Nuns was a very close friend of my old man's sister, Aunt Theresa.

When it became certain that Mama was only going to live for a couple more days, my brother and I were packed up and driven to Aunt Theresa's house. Today the trip would take less than an hour, but back then, on the old high-crown Macadam roads, it took over three hours to get to Saint Louis.

A couple of days before Mama died, my brother and I were taken to the hospital at midnight. Aunt Theresa's friend was working the graveyard shift. After writing that last sentence, I just realized the dark humor it might convey. There is no pun intended, however, and I'll not change it.

Arriving at the hospital, Uncle Herman parked in the back of the building in the "Deliveries Only" area. The Nun met us as the door, told us we had to be exceptionally quiet, and she escorted us to Mama's room.

She had been moved to a very small, private room where she could rest and be allowed to have peace and quiet. When we entered the door, I ran to her in the bed. Harold stood at the end of the bed but I reached up and grabbed hold of Mama and hugged her for all I was worth. I think I may have hurt her, but she didn't say anything.

I can see her lying there, looking very, very tired. She was emaciated and she was in great deal of pain. I kept hugging her and I didn't want to let her go.

Harold came to the other side of the bed and gave her a hug and she put her arms around both of us with the little strength she had left.

We stayed that way for a few moments and then I asked, "Can you come home soon? I've made up some stories to tell you and I've been practicing some songs for you."

The Nun whispered to me that I had to be very quiet and not talk loudly. She said she could get into a lot of trouble if I didn't follow her instructions. I whispered, "Okay, but I want to sing Mama her song."

The Nun said, "If you can sing it in a whisper, it'll be alright, but only sing one verse. Then you're going to have to leave. Your Mama needs her rest."

I very quietly whispered Mama's favorite song, *In The Garden*. When I was done I asked again, "When are you coming home?"

Aunt Theresa said, "Mama's going to stay here for a while longer. We'll talk about it when we get home. We've got to go now. Give Mama a hug and say Goodbye."

That's when I began to cry.

Mama put her hand on my head and said, "Now, Mikey, don't do that. You've got to be a brave little man for me. Always remember that I love you."

I told her I loved her, too. Aunt Theresa and her friend ushered us out of the room.

I remember looking back when we were walking out the door, whispering, "'Bye, Mama. I love you. I hope you can come home soon."

That was the last time I saw Mama. She died the next day. She was embalmed at the hospital and her body was brought back to Flat River. Her funeral services were held at the Esther Baptist Church where she had been a member since 1929.

The little talk that Aunt Theresa was going to have with Harold and me never happened. Not that morning, nor the next day, not ever. Nor did anyone else talk to us about Mama dying. I don't recall anyone ever coming right out and saying she was dead. I heard comments such as, "She's in a better place now," "She's with the angels," "Her spirit is with us," and "She's past suffering now." No one ever came right out and told me she was dead.

I can't imagine that I'll ever forget the funeral.

My old man was nowhere to be found. I looked for him and was unable to find him anywhere. I'm guessing he was in some dark little corner feeling sorry for himself, having lost his wife, and now being saddled with two little kids.

Grandma and Grandpa Province were taking care of Harold and me. Mama's parents, Grandmother and Grand-daddy Criteser ignored us.

I never understood why Mama's casket was closed. From what I could gather, listening to the adults talking, there had been

76

some mix-up, followed by a heated argument between the Provinces and the Critesers, and the casket had been prematurely closed and locked.

Much later in my life I was told that Mama specifically asked Grandma and Grandpa Province to take us in and care for us. She said she did not, under any circumstances, want her mother and father to have custody of us. I have no idea why she said that, I don't know what the problem was with her parents, and I've never found out why. No one would ever tell me.

Just before the services were to begin, I asked if I could please see Mama and was told by someone from the funeral home, "No, you can't. The coffin is shut. Sit down and keep quiet."

I asked Grandma Province, "Why can't I see Mama?" She said it was best that I not see her because she didn't look like Mama anymore. Her explanation was, "Besides, your Mama's spirit is in heaven now."

I gave that some thought and didn't understand it. If she wasn't in the casket, why was the casket there and who was in the casket? I started asking questions and was told repeatedly to be quiet.

The service started, the minister said some nice things about Mama and a few people stood up and told little stories about her. The congregation sang In The Garden and the minister thanked everyone for attending the funeral. That was it.

As the casket was being carried out of

the church, I told Grandma, "I don't understand. Why can't I see Mama?"

When I began to cry, some woman I didn't know picked me up and carried me to a small room in the back of the church. People watched us, shook their heads, made "tsk-tsk" noises, and said things like, "Poor little boy," "He must really miss his mother," and "He'll get over it."

After all the people had gone, Grandma and Grandpa came in, took me by the hand, and walked me to a car. Harold was already inside. I didn't know the person driving the car but they drove Grandma, Grandpa, Harold, and me to our new home on Theodore Street.

My old man was still nowhere to be seen.

The Entertainer

Over my lifetime, I have attempted to expand my interests and abilities.

I've served in the army, had a career in the newspaper industry, and I worked in the computer industry from the ancient punch-card days through the many iterations of computers up to and including today's marvelous machines.

As a community college computer science instructor I wrote my own textbooks.

I've been active in live theater and have appeared on radio and television. I've acted, directed, produced, and written for the theatrical stage.

I adhere to Abraham Maslow's principle of "self-actualization," which he describes as: "What a man can be, he must be. This need we may call self-actualization . . . It refers to the desire for self-fulfillment, namely, to the tendency for him to become actualized in what he is potentially. This tendency might be phrased as the desire to become more and more what one is, to become everything that one is capable of becoming."

I often wonder why I've done all the things I've done and why I continue to do so. What drives me? I'm neither rich nor famous, but I've kept busy. I see other people who do as little as possible and are quite happy about it. I can't seem to do that and I wonder why. I have a theory, but I don't think its something I'll ever be able to validate. It goes like this:

When I was seven years old, Mama died from "uremia." Uremia is an accumulation of urinary waste products in the blood which is caused by renal failure. In short, Mama died of kidney failure. With today's medical knowledge and methods she could be saved, but in 1952 such miracles were unavailable.

I seem to be getting off the subject, so I will return to my little story of "The Entertainer."

Following Mama's death, my old man was having difficulty dealing with the loss of his wife and the responsibility for the two small children she left behind, namely me and my brother Harold. Freddie Lee was grown up and in the army. I found out later the old man was in the care of a psychiatrist for a while during this chapter of our lives. He was an out-patient at the state mental hospital located in Farmington. He was intermittently on medications for a condition called "Melancholia." Today it's called Depression.

Anyway, my old man, my brother, and I moved in with my grandparents; the Province grandparents. I can now understand the inconvenience and nuisance we caused. They were in their late sixties, they had brought up their own children, they had retired, and they wanted peace and quiet. They weren't prepared to take care of a seven year old and a nine year old child.

I must have been more of a problem than Harold because my Grandma always referred to him as "the good boy." Logically, I suppose, that would make me the "the bad boy." I was reminded of this on a regular basis. I got used to it.

It is well known that "bad boys" need lots of additional, special guidance so I was delivered to some nice ladies at the Esther Baptist Church every Sunday so they could mold me into a satisfactory little man.

Thinking back on this episode in my life, I realize that these women knew Mama and they must have been her friends. Mama was a member in good standing at this church from 1929 until her death. From my current viewpoint, I can appreciate that they were nice people and they were simply doing what they thought was best for me.

For over three years, I was sent to church every Sunday. I was put into my little navy blue suit, my white shirt with French-cuffs, my spiffy pre-knotted necktie, and my little-boy wing-tipped shoes were polished to a high luster.

My old man would drive me to the church and dump me at the front steps. After delivering me, his job was done. He would drive off and be gone for the rest of the day. I have no idea where he went nor what he did. Once in a great while he would be waiting outside the church and he'd give me a ride home. Most often, though, he never bothered to pick me up and I'd walk the three miles home.

81

On those rare occasions when he did pick me up, he would drive me home, keep the engine running while I got out of the car, and he would take off again to who knows where. I never saw much of him, but by that time, I didn't care.

My instructions were to enter the church and wait in the vestibule until the "nice church ladies" came by to pick me up. I was then hustled into the church Narthex (the back of the church) which was the Sunday School area where I attended classes on the old-time gospel.

After Sunday School, I was ushered into the church Nave (the middle of the church) where the congregation assembled for the main service. I was placed in the front row so I could receive the full benefit of every sermon. On occasion, when I was to perform, I was seated in the Altar area. Notice how I know all the proper names for the parts of a church. I was instructed on all this and was apparently an apt student.

The church ladies must have had many intense discussions concerning me. It was evident that they had given much consideration to the question of "What will we do with Mikey?" The end result was that they came up with a complete program for me and my enrichment.

I was given lessons to learn, bible verses to memorize, stories to tell, parables to act out, and songs to sing. I became their project. I was to them as clay in the hands of a sculptor. I was to be molded into "The

Church Entertainer."

I acted, I told stories, I explained the mysterious intricacies of the Baptist bible as they had been explained to me, I gave "little boy" sermons, and I sang all the popular hymns. I gave it everything I had.

Now that I think about it, giving it careful consideration, I believe it was the only outlet I had at the time. My grandparents didn't want me around, my old man had no use for me, and my brother was "strange." I, in fact, had no one. Even with the entire congregation in front of me as I performed, I was alone. Please don't misunderstand what I'm saying. I was alone but I was never lonely.

In 1946 *The Jolson Story* made its way to the silver screen. I don't remember seeing the movie, but I remember hearing all of its songs on the radio.

In 1949, *Jolson Sings Again* came out and I do remember seeing that one. I remember seeing it on the big screen and listening to the songs on the radio. I liked that kind of music and I began to memorize many of the songs sung by "Jolie."

On Sundays, I became a miniature Al Jolson. I didn't just sing a song, I "sold" a song. I played it for every tear I could squeeze out of their eyes. I broke my little voice at all the right places and I ripped out their hearts.

I was . . . The Entertainer.

As I run those memories through my mind's eye they seem like scratchy old films. I can see the church, the steps, the alter, the piano, and the weekly attendance sign with hymn numbers assigned for the day. I can hear the piano. It's playing *In The Garden*. Where's my spotlight? I'm ready to perform.

I see a little boy in a navy blue suit at the alter. He looks a lot like me. The church is quiet, the piano begins a soft eight bar introduction, and this one little boy is commanding the attention of the whole congregation.

Sometimes, for effect, I'd "dedicate" a song to the memory of my Mama and I'd watch the old ladies as I sang directly to them. Their lower lips would tremble, they'd bring out their clean, white hankies, and they'd weep softly as I sang. Even at such a young age I understood these things.

> I come to the garden alone,
> While the dew is still on the roses.
> And the voice I hear, falling on my ear,
> The Son of God discloses . . .

Oh, yes, I knew how to play them like a cheap violin. Mess with me, will they? Anyway, that's my theory.

Happy Birthday

I honestly don't care much for birthdays. There are almost seven billion people in the world as I type these words with more being born every single second. Each of those people has a birthday so how important a day can it be? It seems to me that the significance of birthdays is being diluted at an enormous rate.

Or, on the other hand, my poor opinion of birthday celebrations may stem from my experiences while living with my grandparents. Here's the story:

I was born on the 15th of May. My brother, Harold, was born on the 21st of May. When we were much younger, I used to make the lame joke that at least for a few days, he was only one year older than me. Of course, at this point in my life humor was a simplistic thing. To me, a "dirty" joke would be, "A little boy fell into a mud puddle." So much for the sophistication of youthful humor.

My Grandma was a very frugal person. She was always uttering things like, "Waste not, want not." When the month of May came around, as it does every year, she brought her own special brand of thrift to the occasion of our birthdays.

Her plan was remarkably brilliant in its

simplicity. Since both of our birthdays were in May and both of our birthdays were a mere six days apart, it would be absolute nonsense to have two separate parties. The apparent and obvious answer was to have a single party at which we would celebrate both birthdays. Problem solved.

As far as I was concerned, however, this created a certain dilemma. Every year, without fail, the day chosen for the party was always the 21st of May. Never, ever did a birthday party occur on my birthday. I began to fear that some sort of conspiracy might be afoot and I was of the opinion that this arrangement was surprisingly favorable to Harold. But, then, he was the "good boy."

I once questioned Grandma about this. I suggested the idea that it might be fun to have the combined birthdays on the 15th of May, just to see what might happen, just to see if that might be feasible for future celebrations.

Grandma's response was immediate, "We're celebrating both days so what difference does it make?"

I countered this logic with the comment, "Yes, that's what I'm saying. What difference does it make? Why not have it on the 15th this year instead of the 21st?"

She continued the negotiations with the explanation that, "We're having the party on the 21st and that's that. So you can just keep quiet. You don't appreciate anything I do for you, do you?"

I must admit that, at this point, I had

very few chips with which to bargain so I conceded to Grandma's splendidly made argument.

The parties continued to be held on Harold's birthday.

Now I know that no one likes a complainer, but I do think that I should be allowed to make one further comment.

For some inexplicable reason, the kids attending these parties were invariably Harold's friends or classmates and they all had the mistaken impression that it was Harold's party. I became suspicious that something was not quite right when I overheard him telling the kids, "Thanks for coming to my party."

Adding to the basis of my misgivings was the fact that all the presents had his name on them. Again, I apologize for sounding like a complainer, but I don't remember ever receiving a single gift at these parties.

The first couple of years, I asked some of the kids about this. They told me they were told this was Harold's party. After all, they continued, my birthday was last week. Some of them even asked me why I hadn't invited them to my party.

I eventually stopped bothering about it.

I didn't care anymore.

As Grandma said, "What difference does it make?"

Sunset Carson. The cowboy star I met
at the Roseland Theater in Flat River.

Sunset Carson

I love a good movie. There's nothing like a well made film to take my mind off things and ease the burdens of life. My preference is for films with character definition and storylines as opposed to car crashes and things being blown up. That's why I enjoy Shakespeare and have been involved with live theater most of my life; acting singing, producing, directing, and writing plays.

At one point in my life, I had plans to move to California, learn the acting craft at the Pasadena Playhouse, and become a big star. But "things happened" and I never made it to stardom. Tis a pity, indeed.

I'm not a fan of a lot of the movies made these days. Many of them are silly, contrived chick flicks, sophomoric "body noise" flicks, or nothing more than a collection of computer generated graphics.

The thing I find fascinating about motion-pictures is that a good story is always a good story. Many films made in the 1930s, 1940s, and 1950s are as good, if not better than, many films made today.

Titles that come immediately to mind are: *Baby Face, The Public Enemy, Little Caesar, Forty-Second Street, Goodbye Mr. Chips, Twelve O'clock High, Shane, The Umbrellas of*

Cherbourg, *The 400 Blows*, *Repulsion*, *The Godfather*, *The Wild Child*, *It's a Gift*, *Jean de Flourette*, and *The Cowboys*.

I could make a list of my one-hundred favorite films, but this is not the place for that. This is supposed to be a story about meeting movie stars.

When I was living with my grandparents, I spent a lot of time at the Roseland Theater in Flat River. And I mean a LOT of time there. I loved being in the darkened theater with refrigerated air and seeing people I would never meet in real life.

It was not a happy time for us back then. My old man was having problems of his own, he never had time for us, and my grandparents weren't all that thrilled about having to take care of my brother and me.

I did odd jobs around the neighborhood for spare change and I'd always watch for soda bottles on the walk to and from school. Two cents per bottle wasn't too bad back then. Of course in those days, a dime was worth more than one of today's dollars.

On Saturdays, the Roseland Theater had the bargain of a lifetime. For the price of a single ticket, I could see a triple-feature, newsreels, cartoons, the latest installment of a serial, short subjects (*Three Stooges, Behind the Eight Ball, Follow the Bouncing Ball*, etc.) and previews of coming attractions. Taking my time walking to the theater, staying there for five or six hours, and taking more time walking home would fritter away an entire day.

The price of the ticket was ten cents,

plus a Missouri "entertainment tax" of four cents. I never figured out why the state charged four cents tax on a visit to the movie theater. But, then, politicians are all stupid and crazy.

Anyway, with fifteen cents in my pocket, that left me a single penny. Luckily, there was a Lions Club Gumball Machine next to the box office and I would get a piece of gum that usually had to last for the five or six hours I spent in the theater.

On those rare days when I was flush with an additional dime or even a quarter, I could have popcorn, soda, and maybe even a Sugar Daddy. Life was good in the Roseland Theater.

I would sit there waiting for the show to start and when the lights went down, I was enveloped in the darkness and living in a paradise of illusion. I loved the anonymity of the counterfeit night.

The weekly triple-feature was composed of a wide variety of films. The types of movies shown were almost always second or third run films and many of them were ten to twenty years old, but they were still good films and very entertaining.

If the theater did show a "new" movie, it was usually some sort of cheap monster flick aimed at a young audience. They were "B-movies" from a "B-Studio." Films such as; *The Blob, The Attack of the Fifty-Foot Woman, Wasp Woman, It Came From Outer Space*, and *The Amazing Shrinking Man*. Every now and then one of them would even be in 3-D.

Whoever it was at the theater making up the weekly program did a good job of assimilating a combination of film fare such as action, adventure, comedy, crime, gangsters, horror, science-fiction, thrillers, ghost stories, and westerns. Films that were never shown were love stories, historical dramas, and musicals. All in all, it was a sanctuary for a young boy on a Saturday afternoon.

As usual, I'm rambling and not getting to the story. I've been told that if someone asks me what time it is, I'll tell them how a watch is made. So here's the story, which is actually two stories in one:

One Saturday afternoon, I arrived at the theater a little too early. The box office wasn't open yet so I waited in front of the theater, sitting on the steps. I was somewhat amazed to see this huge blue Cadillac park in front of the theater entrance.

The guy getting out of the car was dressed in a cowboy style suit. He was wearing a cowboy tie, cowboy boots, and a large Stetson. He was big, just like his car.

I watched him come up the steps and walk into the lobby. As he went by he looked at me and said, "Hi, there, buddy."

I followed him in the door and I saw him shake hands with the manager, talking to him for a few minutes before handing him a box. Then he turned to leave.

Seeing me there, he stopped and said, "Hello, again, young man, How are you today?" I said, "I'm just fine, sir. You look familiar."

He laughed, put his hand out (which I shook) and he said, "I'm glad you recognize me. My name's Forrest Tucker. I've been doing some work in Saint Louis and I'm just passing through Flat River. I stopped by to give the manager here a box of signed pictures to give away when my new movie starts here Friday."

He half-turned toward the manager, saying, "Make sure my little pardner here gets one of those pictures." The manager said, "Yes, sir, Mr. Tucker, I certainly will."

He turned back to me and said, "You don't have to call me Mr. Tucker. You can call me Forrest." I replied, "Yes, sir. Thank you . . . Forrest." We shook hands again.

Watching him leave, I must have had a large grin on my face. I found out later that Forrest Tucker was six-feet, six-inches tall, two-inches taller than John Wayne. With his boots on, to a little kid, he looked like he was about ten feet tall. He was a very nice guy.

Years later, during my senior year in high school, our drama club went to Saint Louis to see the opening performance of the "American Theater."

The theater was built in 1917, had become a burlesque house, had fallen into disrepair, and finally had been refurbished.

The first show at the newly renovated theater was *The Music Man* starring my old pal Forrest Tucker. He was Professor Harold Hill, the role made famous by Robert Preston on Broadway. I've seen the movie and comparing it with the live stage version, I can safely say that Forrest Tucker was just as good as

Robert Preston.

Since it was the first night of the production and because we had come such a distance, Mr. Tucker, graciously came to the lobby after the performance and discussed the play with us. I think it surprised everyone when I told him about our first meeting and he said he remembered me.

The other movie star I met at the Roseland Theater was a cowboy star named Sunset Carson.

His real name was Winifred Maurice Harrison but it was changed to Sunset Carson by Lou Grey who ran Republic Pictures in the 1940s. Grey also started the "story" that Sunset Carson was related to the real life Kit Carson.

Carson was a rodeo rider in his youth and he worked in a western show owned by Tom Mix. He signed a contract with Republic Pictures in 1944 and within two years he was one of the top ten money makers in cowboy movies. His horse was named Cactus.

I not only got to meet him, I "performed" with him.

There had been an advertisement in the *Daily Journal* that Sunset Carson would be making an appearance at the Roseland Theater and I was determined to see him.

The big day finally arrived and I was at the theater about an hour early, just to make sure I got a good seat. I even wore my cowboy hat for the occasion. It was a cheap, white knock-off of a Stetson, but I thought it gave me a certain flair, a "Je ne sais quoi."

The last movie of the afternoon's triple feature was the one with Sunset Carson. I don't even remember the name of the movie, but I sure remember what happened after "The End" showed up on the big silver screen.

The theater manager came out onto the stage, bringing a microphone and a small table with him. In those days, theater screens still had stages in front of them for occasional live performances. He thanked everyone for showing up and then introduced, "Sunset Carson," who walked out from behind the large movie screen to a huge round of applause from all of us kids in the audience. He was wearing his special white buckskin outfit with the special boots he had made just for these occasions. I thought to myself, "This is better than being a lead miner."

He introduced himself, talked about Hollywood and the movie industry for a while, told us some stories about things that happened while he was making movies and then he said he had something special to show us.

On the table next to him, rested a gun case. He opened it and took out an exquisitely beautiful .22 rifle. It had a pearlized plastic stock that positively shimmered under the theater lights. It was mesmerizing.

He told us it was a semi-automatic and it had been made especially made for him. At that moment, I no longer wanted my BB gun. I wanted a pearlized semi-automatic .22 rifle.

I'm telling you, it was the most magnificent piece of weaponry I had ever seen.

It was a unique blue-steeled beauty and every kid in the audience wanted one, too.

Holding the rifle gently, affectionately in the crook of his arm, he looked out at the audience and said, "I need a volunteer." There was an eruption of hoots and hollers. Every kid in the audience wanted the job. He looked us over and then said, "That young man right there. The one with the white Stetson. Come on up her, pal."

I could hardly believe that he had chosen me. When I got onto the stage about a quarter-second later, he said, "The reason I chose this young man is because he's wearing a white hat. Everybody knows that only good guys wear white hats."

Then he shook my hand and told me what he wanted me to do. There was a large, very thick block of wood stuck on top of a pole on the stage with us. He explained that he was going to give me a target to hold. I was to stand very still and hold the target against the block of wood so he could shoot it. This was getting better by the minute.

He loaded the .22 rifle. He walked all the way to the back of the theater. He yelled out for me to hold up the target and not to move.

Blam, blam, blam, blam, blam.

Blam, blam, blam, blam, blam.

Ten shots!

Ten bull's-eyes!

It was magnificent!

He came back to the stage, took the target from me and signed it. Then he asked if

I would help him hand out some autographed photographs. I said, "You betcha I will."

We went back to the theater lobby and he shook hands with every kid in the theater as they left. He took the time to talk with each and every one of them. I stood next to him and handed a photograph to every kid.

I kept that target and his autographed photograph for years, but disasters happen. Upon graduating from high school and joining the army, my grandma threw away all of the things that I had stored in her basement.

I miss that autographed Sunset Carson target with all the bull's-eyes.

I think about it more often than I probably should.

With the little girls next door, 1947.
I don't remember their names, but
the one sitting next to me was
always kissing me.

No Sissies Allowed

I heard on the news that some schools have outlawed Dodge Ball because "someone might get hurt." For crying out loud, what has happened to this country? Where's the tough pioneer spirit? Where's the rugged individualism that carved a nation out of the wilderness? Is the next generation going to be raised as sissies?

Children can't ride bicycles without helmets, knee pads, elbow pads, and pads for the pads. Where will it all stop?

Playgrounds are covered with thick foam padding so the kiddies won't fall off a swing and hurt themselves. I once saw a mother putting a bicycle helmet on her kid before letting him on the swing set.

I wonder how I ever made it through childhood without all this protection. It must have been a miracle. When I was a kid we were allowed to be kids. We were told to get out of the house and go play somewhere.

During recess at school, we used the swings to see how high we could go. We had contests to see who could jump furthest off the swings.

We played Dodge Ball with an absolute vengeance. The whole idea was to smack someone with the ball hard enough to knock them off their feet. We loved it.

Playgrounds were covered with gravel or blacktop and when you landed hard, sometimes it hurt. You were expected to get a bump, a bruise, or an abrasion of some sort. If it didn't bleed, it wasn't worth mentioning.

Everyone has heard the proverbial warning about BB guns: "You'll shoot your eye out, kid." I defy anyone reading this to name a single individual they personally knew who really did get an eye shot out. It's one of those improvable and untraceable urban legends.

Up the street from my grandparents home was a decrepit, dilapidated old house that always looked like it was on the verge of collapse. My BB gun pals and I used that house for our BB gun fights, hunting each other from room to room. At worst, one of us might get a few welts but we never whined about it. Whining was, and is, for sissies.

There was this one time I was shooting my BB gun through an old drain pipe just to hear the ricochet. My "peculiar" older brother told me not to do that. He put his hand in front of the pipe thinking it would stop me. I told him he'd better move his hand but he didn't. I cocked the gun, held the barrel about an inch from his hand and pulled the trigger. Then I laughed. He was given ample warning. He could have moved his hand. He cried all the way to Grandma's house and I eventually got a whipping but so what? It was no big deal.

There are "professional" bike riders and skate boarders today who perform all sorts of amazing aerial and acrobatic tricks. In my day, we lacked the "technology" to perform these swell tricks. Our old, heavy Schwinn bikes were way to clunky and bulky for the feats of aerodynamic maneuvers we envisioned, but we tried.

I was never able to become airborne long enough to make a full somersault, but I gave it all I had. I got my share of bumps and bruises, but that was the price you paid.

When I played football in high school we used old leather football helmets. It wasn't until much later that the school could afford plastic helmets resembling jet pilot headgear.

We wore wool uniforms with some so-called padding in the shoulders and that was all the protection we had. Our shoes were the high-top lace-up type with steel spikes riveted onto the soles and heels. It could be pretty nasty if you got spiked, but if someone did spike you, they knew that you would most certainly return the favor. Tit for tat.

We had no such thing as shoulder pads, thigh pads, and all that other fancy stuff. Sure, we got knocked around, but no one died.

Emerson Hill was about a quarter mile long and all downhill. And when I say downhill, by golly, I mean downhill. It must have been at least a thirty percent grade. It wasn't only difficult to walk up Emerson Hill, it gave new meaning to the word treacherous after a snowstorm. Even on a nice, warm day a car would have a hard time driving up the hill unless it had a solid transmission. It was the type of hill a Model-T would have to go up in reverse.

All the kids in the neighborhood knew that Emerson Hill was the best place in town for sledding. Our old Flexible Flyer's were supposed to be "steerable" but in reality steering was merely a suggestion. They went where they wanted to go.

One of my pals, his name was David, was about a third of the way down the hill when his sled caught a rough patch that was melting and he lost control of his sled. He veered off to the left and into a drainage ditch. His sled went one way and he went another, ending up head first into a bunch of large rocks.

He laid there for a minute and we all ran to see if he was alive. When he finally got to his feet he was crying. The jagged rock he ran into had torn off his knit cap and ripped a large gash on the top of his head. His head and face were covered in blood. With that much blood, it was okay to cry.

I took the big, red handkerchief out of my pocket, folded it into a square, and put it on his head. We put his knit cap back on his head to hold the handkerchief in place.

Holding his cap and the handkerchief, and dragging his sled, he started home.

We watched him for a minute and someone called out, "See ya in school tomorrow," but he missed school the next day.

The day after that, though, he showed up with a huge scab and a lot of stitches on his head. He showed everybody his wound, even let us feel it, and we were all very envious of him. I suppose today he would be kept in the hospital for a few days "for observation" and it would cost thousands of dollars. Back then, the doctor probably charged fifty bucks or so.

Speaking of hospital bills, I had my appendix removed when I was eleven years old. I came home the day after the operation and the whole thing cost around a hundred and thirty dollars.

Now that I think about David and his accident, I realize that I never got my handkerchief back.

Freddie and me on his bicycle, 1947 or '48.
It was all the rage to remove the chain guard
from bicycles then. Oh, my goodness, we're
not wearing helmets or protective gear.
We'll all be killed.

Christmas With Grandma

I am fully cognizant that Christmas is for celebrating the birth of Jesus Christ. As a Christian would say, "Jesus is the reason for the season."

Unfortunately, when you're a little kid, some of the intricate distinctions between faith and childish greed can easily become blurred and obfuscated.

Every year, Grandma would receive a Sears-Roebuck mail order catalogue and at the first chance, I would thumb through the big book, going directly to the toy section. I was enthralled by the new and wonderful selection of things that were available to make a kid's life worth living. I was well aware of the minuscule likelihood of me actually getting anything that I really wanted, but as politicians will have us believe, "Hope springs eternal," and I eternally hoped.

Of course, Harold and I always received our requisite and obligatory shares of underwear and socks. I even received the occasional, spiffy pre-knotted tie to go with my little navy blue suit.

But, one year, I remember, was especially appalling and loathsome.

When children are reared by grandparents, something remarkable occurs.

Mind you that animals are raised, children are reared. Anyway, those children are brought up being taught values that are neither analogous nor parallel to contemporary "modern" principles and standards.

The values taught to Harold and to me were those held by two people born in the 1880s and our upbringing reflected those "old-fashioned" morals and beliefs.

We were taught to say, "Yes, Sir" and "Yes, Ma'am." Strict adherence to the distinct conviction that children should be seen and not heard was paramount in Grandma's household. Speaking back, or being "sassy," brought quick and terrible retribution at the wrong end of a switch or razor strap.

The esoteric concepts of which I speak, however, have only clarified themselves as I move through the aging process, gaining wisdom with every passing year.

Years ago I would have made the comment that, "I fear I am becoming my Grandfather," but as time passes, I realize that may not be such a bad thing. I accept and welcome the notion.

Having said this, however, I must make the comment that I would never, under any circumstances, do what my Grandmother did to me on one certain Christmas. What she did was devastating to my little psyche.

This particular Christmas had started out pretty swell and I had reason to hope that it might even get better. Grandma had even "gotten with the program" and bought one of those new aluminum Christmas trees. Going the whole distance, she even acquired the little spotlight with the multi-colored rotating disk that gave the shiny man-made tree a variation of color schemes never before imagined.

The truth is this; the tree was nothing more than a long, thick pole with wooden dowels inserted into drilled holes. It was painted silver. The "branches" were covered with cheap twirled pieces of aluminum. It was far from being impressive; not quite what I had imagined it to be. Harold, of course, loved it because it was shiny and flashy.

Christmas morning started out okay and I was looking forward to at least one or two spiffy presents from good old Santa Claus.

I had carefully handled and assessed each present and opened the ones I knew were the socks, underwear, and other sundry pieces of clothing. I was now on the verge of preparing to get my little hands on "the good stuff."

The first big box I picked up was substantial. I could tell there was something important inside. It was the size of an oversized shoebox and my fevered little brain was hoping that my heavy-handed hints had worked.

When I tore off the wrapping paper, I froze for just a few seconds. It was a shoe box with pictures of cowboy boots on it. These, however, were not just "cowboy" boots. These were the epitome of cowboy boots. They were manufactured as a special "one-time-only" offering made exclusively by Red Goose Shoes for this Christmas season.

They were exactly like the boots worn by "The King of the Cowboys," Roy Rogers. They had his unique "double eagles" on the back of each boot and there was a picture of Roy, himself, smiling at me from the top of the box. This, my friend, is what Christmas is all about.

I carefully removed the box top and took the boots out. In my excitement, I was not paying a lot of attention as I put them on and when I stood up I realized the horror of what had been done to my boots.

Grandma had taken the brand new boots to a shoe shop where she had the cowboy heels ripped off and replaced with plain, flat rubber heels made for regular street shoes.

I stood there, looking at the boots. I was confused and baffled, trying to make sense of this folly, this madness. I looked at Grandma and asked her, "What did you do to these boots?" Her feeble response was, "Well, the heels were too high for you. I had them replaced with flat heels so you could walk in them."

I was crushed, hurt, humiliated, annoyed, angry, and other things I can't even say. My boots were ruined. As I stood there, the boots mocked me. They looked like something that would be worn by an evil genie out of Ali Baba and the Forty Thieves. The only things missing were the little bells on the ends of the toes that pointed almost straight in the air.

To top off the utter humiliation of the moment, I could hardly stand up straight in those butchered boots. I was ashamed to even be seen in them. I took them off, put them back in the box, swallowed my shame, and (as I had been taught) said, "Thank you."

I sat there on the floor for a minute, until Grandma said, "I think there's one more present there for you."

Moving slowly, as if in a dream, I listlessly reached over and picked the last present with my name on it. It was in a small box and I had no idea what it was. I hadn't asked for anything except the cowboy boots.

I looked at the package in my hands and thought, "At least it can't be a ruined pair of Roy Rogers boots. How bad can it be?" And then I discovered just how bad it could be.

I lethargically tore the paper away and looked at the pretty pink box. I'll say it again: pretty pink box. Fearing the worst, I opened it and took out the wallet inside. I almost cried. I wanted to throw it at Grandma. Oh, yes, it was a wallet, but it was a girls wallet. And it was a pink girls wallet.

Now let me explain something. A boys wallet is simply a couple pieces of leather sewn together. It folds over and you can put paper money in it. That's it. That's all. It isn't supposed to be anything more than that. Simplicity, thy name is boys wallet.

The wallet I held in my hands resembled a boys wallet only in the sense that it could be folded. Did I mention that it was pink? It had a snap that folded over the end of the wallet to keep it closed. It had a little coin purse inside. It had an accordion-like folder for lots of pictures. It had a pretty little stamped flower design on the outside. It was pink.

I put it back into its box and again (as I had been taught) said, "Thank you."

When everyone's presents had been opened, and the wrapping paper had been cleaned up, I took my spoiled, ruined, mangled boots and my pink wallet to my bedroom. I threw them under the bed. I neither looked at them nor touched them again. For all I know, they were there when Grandpa died and the house was sold.

I did mention that the wallet was pink, didn't I?

Merry Christmas.

Working On Grandpa's Farm

During the years my brother and I were living with our grandparents, we spent every summer on their farm.

Grandpa owned two hundred acres a few miles from the little town of Irondale, Missouri and after retiring from the lead mines, he spent as much time as possible on his farm.

When the school year ended, we packed up everything we needed and moved to the farm until the school year resumed.

Grandpa's farm was surrounded by other Province farms; Uncle Marion, Uncle Frank, Uncle William, and others I don't even remember. At one time, Provinces owned just about everything in the area for miles around. Little by little, however, I think the farms have been sold off. I wonder if any of the land in the area is still owned by anyone with the name of Province. I haven't been back there for a very long time so I don't know.

Having just done an internet search, I've found that County Road 520 is still referred to as Province Road on the maps.

The house we lived in was old and shabby, never had plumbing, but it had a decent roof. My Grandpa was born in this house in 1886. I'm certain the house was built well before the Civil War. It had a root cellar and a kitchen with an old wood-burning cook stove. In addition to cooking our meals, the reservoir on the side of the stove provided the only hot water we had.

On the bottom floor, there was a front room, a dining room, and a bedroom with two beds. Grandpa and Grandma shared one bed and my brother and I shared the other one. There was also a large, screened in front porch where we would sit in the evenings and watch the stars move across the sky.

The second story of the house was separated into two large rooms accessible by an extremely steep and narrow staircase. These rooms were only used if relatives came to visit. I would never go up there because of the "mud daubers" that made their nests in the eves.

Grandpa told me that "mud daubers" were "good wasps" because they killed black and brown spiders, which could give you a nasty bite. He also told me the mud daubers would never sting you. That turned out to be a lie.

I was told to sweep the floors in both upper rooms one day because Aunt Theresa was coming for a visit. I was minding my own business, I didn't bother the mud daubers in any way, but they still stung me about a half a dozen times. After that I refused to go up there.

I informed Grandpa that he could strap me all day long if he wanted to, but "You're not gonna get me up there again."

Besides the wasps, we had a family of skunks living under the house but Grandpa left them alone. Skunks really aren't the bothersome animals some people think they are. They're actually just a member of the ferret family and if you leave them alone, they'll leave you alone.

On occasion there may have been a very slight odor from them, but for the most part they ignored us. To this day, every time I get a whiff of skunk I have flashbacks to the days on the farm and the old farmhouse.

Upon arriving at the house in the summer, the first job assigned to me was to get out the ladder, go around the entire house, top to bottom, and pound in the nails that were sticking out. The nails holding the house together were not the nice galvanized ones you buy at a hardware store today. They were "blacksmith" nails; handmade one at a time using a forge and anvil. I should have saved some of them. I understand they are very collectible these days.

Until the last year we lived with my grandparents, we had no electricity in the house. Also, no indoor plumbing. There was a spring about a quarter mile from the house and it was my daily job to bring four buckets of water from the spring for us to use. The old joke about "Saturday night baths" might seem funny to people with good plumbing, but to me Saturday always meant extra trips to the spring for bath water. Grandma always got first crack at the hot water, Grandpa next, then Harold, and finally me. Some things about the "good old days" were not so good.

Our two-holer outhouse was about a hundred yards from the house near the corn crib. I was ten years old when Grandpa decided it was time to dig a new "disposal area" for the outhouse and I was assigned to the job. As I removed each shovelful of dirt from the new hole, I tossed it into the old hole. When the new hole was deep enough, we used a rope to drag the outhouse over the new hole and it was ready to go. Grandpa gave me the privilege of christening the project. Now that I think of it, that was the first plumbing job I ever did.

It may seem odd to folks today that a little, ten year old boy would be required to do such hard work, but that's the way things are on a farm and it's always been that way. Children were given chores to do and they were expected to do them. Moreover, they were expected to do them without complaint.

At the ripe old age of eight, Grandpa took me to the old barn where he kept his two workhorses, Dolly and Daisy. Both horses were large mares, Dolly was white and Daisy was grey. Each of them stood about sixteen hands high.

Although it was difficult, and I had to use a stool, Grandpa taught me how to harness the mares, hitch them to our wagon, and how to drive the team. I still smile when I think about those horses. It instilled a great sense of pride in me to be able to do that at such a young age.

Today's city kids could learn a lot by

having to work on a farm. Instead of the "Peace Corps" perhaps we should create a "Farm Corps." It would do a lot of good for American kids. Charity begins at home, ya know.

I learned a lot on that farm and one of the hardest lessons learned was; "Never name anything you're going to eat."

The first year on the farm I carried shucked corn in my pocket for the little pigs that followed me around. They were not only cute, they were extremely smart, and they loved to have their heads and bellies scratched. When they got to be a certain age, however, they were sold to other farmers for slaughter. Ham and bacon doesn't grow on trees.

Grandpa always kept one pig for our own use and it was pretty rough to see the animal you played with being butchered. As Grandpa said, "Lessons hard learned are lessons well learned."

Another hard learned lesson was; Always wear shoes. I had a habit of going barefoot the first couple of years I was on the farm unless I was working, which seemed to be most of the time. But, when I went for a swim in the creek down the hill from the house, I went without shoes.

One ill-fated day, my Uncle Marion drove his Ford tractor down to our place and he trimmed the sides of the gravel road coming from the main road up to the house. It was a huge device attached to the side of the tractor and it worked just like a hedge trimmer. It was large, noisy, dangerous, and it cut down everything up to an inch thick.

I was walking back from the creek with Harold and my cousin Doris when I started to walk through the path he had cut.

That's when I got stuck, literally stuck. My left foot wouldn't move. I looked down and saw a big bump on the top of my foot where a small tree stump had punctured my foot and was almost all the way through. I had to pull my foot straight up to get it off the little stump and then it started bleeding.

I limped the rest of the way to the farmhouse and stayed outside on the small porch while Harold went in and told Grandma about my predicament. I didn't go inside because if I bled on her floor I knew she would be upset.

Sitting on the steps of the porch, I held my foot up while Grandma gathered what she called "some fixatives." She came out, doused my wound with White Mule, stuffed some cotton in it, and wrapped it up.

White Mule was a concoction invented by Doc Jones, the St. Joe Lead Company doctor. It was made of alcohol, mentholated oil, iodine, and who knows what else. All the miners had ample supplies of it. It was a miracle product that worked on just about anything.

There was no running to the doctor, no tetanus shot, no sympathy, and no complaining. We were a long way from town and we were on our own. Grandpa and Grandma expected us to tough it out.

116

I might mention here that this is the way Grandpa and Grandma grew up and it was how they reared my brother and me. They didn't know any other way.

Grandpa was one of eighteen children. They lived on this farm and they grew up with the bare necessities. His father lost his first wife when she was thirty-one years old. His second wife was Grandpa's mother.

After Grandpa left the farm and married Grandma, he got a job in the lead mines to make a living. He worked on "the trapeze," which was a series of wooden slats hung from the top of a mine shaft with steel hooks. It was the most dangerous job in the mines and it required a lot of strength and nerve. Only a certain type of man could do it and Grandpa was one of those men. My old man couldn't do it; he stayed on the ground. I couldn't do it and I'd never try.

Trapeze miners would walk swinging "bridges" (often one or two hundred feet above the "floor" of the mine) with pole drills on their backs. They drilled holes into the rock, tamped in sticks of dynamite, and then they'd run like hell after lighting a long fuse to detonate the dynamite. They blew out tons of ore this way. It was not a job for anyone with a fear of heights or for the fainthearted. If you look up the word "tough" in the dictionary, you might see a picture of my Grandpa. He was as hard as nails.

It was impossible not to know when a shift change was taking place in the mines. No matter where you were in town, you could hear and feel the substantial thump, thump, thump as each charge of dynamite was set off.

I'm getting off track, let's get back to the farm and my bleeding foot.

For the next few days, my Grandpa would massage my foot and squeeze the hell out of the wound until it bled. He said the sight of rich, red blood was a good sign, meaning that there was no infection.

When it started to scab over and heal, he stopped his "medical procedure" and it mended without further problems.

I can't help but think that today there would be a trip to a doctor or hospital, blood tests, maybe X-rays or an MRI, perhaps a 911 call, and God knows what else. Our country has become a nation of wimps.

I always chuckle when I drive by somebody's place and see them out working their itty-bitty gardens. Grandpa had a fenced-in acre of land next to our farmhouse and this was my grandparents "garden." An acre, for crying out loud. That's about the size of a football field.

We worked the garden with the horses and I was expected to help keep it up. We had corn, tomatoes, potatoes, onions, beets, celery, watermelon, cantaloupe, green beans, peas, carrots, turnips, and other "occasional" crops. We even had a small stand of "popcorn" corn and peanuts.

When we began to harvest from the garden, I would bring in a huge load of wood and Grandma would start the kitchen stove going in preparation for the canning process.

She canned enough to feed an army but instead of keeping all of it, we shared it with relatives in the area. They, in return, shared other farm products with us.

One year on the farm, I was given a puppy by my Uncle Marion. I loved that little dog. He was a smart little guy. One evening I noticed that he hadn't come home for his supper and I began to wonder where he was.

Just before dusk, a stranger drove up the road, stopping next to the fence gate. He wouldn't come inside the yard. He just hollered to see if anyone was home. He said he saw a small dog lying on the edge of the county road and he thought it might be ours.

I ran down to the road to see if it was my pup and, unfortunately, it was. Someone hit him but didn't bother to stop. Grandpa walked down to the road and looked at him. He picked him up by the hind legs and threw him into the ditch on the other side of the road saying, "It ain't no use now. Git on up to the house."

With tears in my eyes, I said, "But I thought I saw him moving." Grandpa looked at me, shook his head, and said, "It ain't nuthin' but his nerves jumpin'. He's dead and you better git over it right here and now. Animals die on a farm and that's the way it is."

He put his arm around my shoulders and walked back to the house with me. Going through the gate he said, "You gotta learn that some things in life hurt and there ain't no gittin' around it. The quicker you understand that, the better off you'll be. I've lost animals, pets, brothers, sisters, and parents. You've already lost yer Mother so you can appreciate that it never gits easier, but life goes on."

Life sure is full of lessons.

Speaking of pets, my cousin, Doris lived just up the road from us. She was Uncle Frank's niece and she was a lot better at being a "farm girl" than I was at being a "farm boy." She was born on the farm and she lived there year-round.

Doris had cut a coupon out of a comic book and sent it, along with twenty-five cents, to a company in Florida. About a week later, her baby alligator arrived. At first it was fun to play with. It's little teeth weren't big enough to hurt anyone.

She kept that reptile for a few years and the last time I saw it, she was keeping it in a large feed trough in the attic. It had grown to three feet in length and it had become very dangerous. She wrote a letter to the folks at the Saint Louis zoo and one day a truck arrived at their house to pick up the alligator.

I've read that alligators in captivity can live to be as much as eighty years old. If that's the case, Doris' alligator may still be alive and living the good life in the Saint Louis zoo.

While we're on the subject of reptiles, I have a little story to share about snakes, cottonmouths to be specific. Some folks call them water-moccasins.

We had copperheads and cottonmouths on the farm and down near the creeks and rivers. Both varieties are mean, vicious, and they're not afraid of people.

One day I was crossing the two-by-four bridge across the creek from our road to the county road and I noticed a large, fat cottonmouth lying on a rock sunning itself; at least so I thought.

I want to make if thoroughly understood that I really hate snakes. I was bitten by a blacksnake once and it was far from an enjoyable experience. Lucky for me that blacksnakes are not poisonous, but anything with teeth can and will bite.

The blacksnake not only bit me, it wouldn't let go. I had to grab it by the head and pull it's teeth out of my hand. Like Grandpa had taught me, I squeezed my hand until it bled really well and it healed without any problems.

That's another case of lessons hard learned being well learned. Never reach for anything in a dark hole unless you know what's in there. For that same reason, I don't like root cellars.

Back to the cottonmouth.

I very quietly walked to the side of the road and picked up the largest rock that I could lift. I carried it over to the bridge and very, very carefully held it until I was sure where it would drop. I let go of the rock and it smashed the snake on its nasty head. While it was struggling, trying to get out from under the rock, I dropped another on its body and almost chopped it into. That's when the most interesting thing happened. That's when I learned that some snakes give birth to live baby snakes. When I asked Grandpa about it, he said all vipers give birth to live baby snakes.

When I split the snake open about a dozen tiny, little snakes came wriggling out of the mother snake's gut. She was birthing them when I happened along. I grabbed as many rocks as I could and began throwing at the malevolent, slimy little creatures. I killed almost all of them but a couple did get away.

I've been told that baby snakes are more dangerous than adult snakes. I don't know how true that is, but they are born fully formed with all the capabilities of an adult snake. They are capable of biting and killing. Until they learn to regulate their bite, they inject all of their venom in a single bite. At least that's what I was told as a kid.

It may be noticed that I haven't mentioned my brother to a large degree in this little story. Grandma never expected nor asked him to do the type of things required of me. He was "different" and he spent most of his time in the house with Grandma. He helped her with the housework and other chores.

Although I never moved west with the original pioneers, I think I have a pretty good idea how children lived in those times.

The Step-Mother

Certain things just stick in a person's mind. The Kennedy killing, the cowardly Muslim attack on the World Trade Center, you know, those kind of things. People tend to remember where they were and what they were doing at those defining moments in time.

One of the occurrences wedged into my brain is my initial meeting with my old man's girl friend, the dim-wit who would become my "step-mother."

Why he married such an enormously obtuse woman just boggles my mind. And, if you've ever had your mind boggled, you'll know what I'm talking about. She was like a cow; she wouldn't walk around a puddle of water if the shortest route was through the puddle.

Here's the story:

The basketball regional finals were in progress at the newly completed field house at Flat River's Central School and Junior College. I wanted to see the games that night because the Crystal City team would be playing.

Crystal City was a small town almost considered a suburb of Saint Louis and there was a young player on the team I wanted to see. We had heard a lot of conjecture that he would play professionally one day.

The kid's name was Bill Bradley and he was, indeed, an exceptional player. He ended his college career as a three-time All-American at Princeton, he spent two years at England's Oxford University on a Rhodes scholarship, and on his return to the U.S. he joined the New York Knicks, playing on their championship teams of 1970 and 1973. He spent his full ten year career with the Knicks and then served three terms as a U.S. Senator for the state of New Jersey. And there I was, watching him play high school basketball.

A friend of mine, a kid named Ray, and I were dropped off at the field house by my old man before the games were to begin. We watched all the games, hung around for awhile, and then meandered outside where we waited in the chilly fall weather for my old man to pick us up. As usual, he was late.

As he pulled up to the curb I started to get into the front seat but when I opened the door I noticed that someone was already sitting there. Some dopey looking broad.

So I opened the back door and got into the backseat, as did Raymond. He looked at me and quietly "mouthed" the words, "Who's she," pointing at her. I shrugged and indicated that I didn't have a clue who she was. Her only remark was, "Can we go now? I have to work tomorrow."

Before we drove off, my old man looked in the rear view mirror saying, "This is Ellen. She's a friend of mine."

She didn't bother to turn around. She just sat there sucking on her cigarette. I almost thought I heard her say, "Hi," but I must have been mistaken.

The ride home was quiet. We stopped at Ray's house and dropped him off, then we went to Grandma's house where I was dropped off. No one said, "Goodbye." Not a word was spoken. I got out, closed the door, and went straight into the house.

I could easily end this story now, but I won't. There's more to tell. Most certainly, there is much more to tell.

For the next couple of weeks I don't remember seeing the old man at all. He apparently went to work, came home to change clothes, and then he left for who knows where. But, then, that was pretty normal, that was his modus operandi.

He came home from work one day and announced that he was taking a vacation. Grandma asked where he was going and he said he wasn't sure but he'd be gone for a couple of weeks. We watched as he got into the car and drove off. The truth is, no one cared where he went. He was never around anyway so what was the difference? Life went on for the next two weeks and then it happened.

Grandma had gotten a phone call from the old man with instructions. We were all supposed to be together in the living room for his arrival in about half an hour. He had an announcement. We gathered and waited.

About an hour and a half later, we saw him drive up and we could see he wasn't alone. Both he and Ellen got out and started for the front door. No one had a clue what this was all about, but I had a really bad feeling about it.

They walked into the living room and stood there for a few moments. He looked at Harold. He looked at me. He said, "Well, kids, meet your new mother!"

I always thought I was a pretty tough little guy, but when he said that, I felt like someone had just punched the guts out of me. Grandma, Grandpa, Harold and I all looked at each other. Grandma's single remark was, "Oh, really?"

Harold, who was always highly excitable, began making sounds that sounded like snarling. His asthma kicked in and he began to have trouble breathing. When he could get a breath he screamed, "She's not my mother. How can you say that? My mother's dead and I wish you were, too."

All in all, it was rather unpleasant. Angry, loud words were screamed more than spoken.

During a lull in the screaming, the old man put his "I don't give a damn" look on his face and said, "Everybody can just shut the hell up. We're married and that's that. You better get your little asses used to it. We're moving out of here."

Unfortunately he failed to think things through, which was par for the course.

Our house on First Street was occupied by renters. They had a lease so they didn't have to leave until the start of the school year.

Grandma announced very clearly that, "That idiot woman can stay in my house when Hell is frozen solid."

Grandpa added, "Amen."

Lastly, Ellen was living in her mother's very small house in Irondale, along with her half-wit daughter and two grandchildren.

It appeared that we had no place to go.

While we waited for the renters to vacate our house, the old man finally decided that it would be best for Harold and me to move out of Grandma's house. I failed to understand his logic. Instead of letting us stay there until we could move into our own house, he said we had to go to Irondale and live with Ellen's family. It was one of his less intelligent decisions.

And that, in a nutshell, was how we left Grandma's house and it was the last time we lived together under the same roof. Previous to this repulsive little episode in my life, Grandpa, Grandma, Harold, and I had all spent the summer months between school years working on Grandpa's farm but that ended right then and there.

Some background information would be helpful at this point.

Ellen was whoring around when she was quite young and by the time she was out of high school she had two daughters. With the first one, the pregnancy did not go well and the girl came out messed up. Her right leg and right arm were much shorter than her left side appendages. If that weren't bad enough, she had an I.Q. of about fifty.

Following family tradition, Ellen's daughters were also sexually active early in their adolescence and they both had children at a very young age. Because of her family's propensity for premature pregnancies, the end result was that Ellen's grandson was the same age as me. Go figure.

We were all squeezed into Ellen's mother's house like sardines.

It was simply splendid.

The daughter ran a beauty parlor out of the living room and the whole house was constantly consumed with the stink of permanent wave chemicals.

To worsen matters, they all smoked like furnaces. The old lady, Ellen's mother, smoked *Kools*, one of the nastiest brands on the market; she burned through three packs of those evil coffin nails every day. The daughter smoked, Ellen smoked, and even the grandchildren were allowed to smoke, but only mentholated brands, of course, because Ellen said they were more healthy for young people.

Harold and I were allowed to have one bath a week so we didn't use up all their hot water. It was explained to us that hot water cost money and the water belonged to Ellen's family anyway. We were informed on a regular basis that we were very lucky to have a place to live.

I was in the General Store of the little town one day and Lenny (the grandson who was my age) came in the store. He asked the storekeeper to make him a bologna sandwich and he asked me if I wanted one. I said,

"Sure, if you're paying for it." He was in an expansive mood that day and said, "We've got an account here." What I didn't know was that the account was for his Great Grandma (the *Kool* smoker) and she never developed a great liking for me.

When I got back to the house that evening, I was confronted by the old lady. She called me a thief, a crook, and a little bastard. She said she had called the local constable and reported me for stealing from her General Store account. She threatened to have me thrown in jail. Everybody in the room thought it was pretty funny. Lenny was laughing the hardest.

Early the next day, I walked to the store and explained things to the storekeeper. He allowed me to sweep out the store to pay for the sandwich. He phoned the old lady and told her that the sandwich was no longer on her bill. I thanked him and left.

From that day on, as long as we were forced to live in Irondale, I left the house as early as possible and returned as late as possible. That lasted for almost three months.

After the "sandwich affair" I never ate or drank anything in that house. I made a deal with the storekeeper who let me work off a sandwich and a soda every day. I never bothered to tell the old man about it.

Finally, when the school year was getting near, the renters moved out of our house and we were able to leave Irondale. Things were slightly better back in Flat River. I was able spend a lot of time at school or at

Grandma's house when things got a bit rough. We still had to endure Ellen, her stupidity, and her incessant chain smoking, but you can't have everything, can you?

At least the house didn't stink of permanent wave chemicals. On the other hand, it did smell like an ash tray.

Just for the heck of it, perhaps I should give two little examples of "Ellen-isms."

She never cooked anything other than fried foods, keeping an iron skillet and large can of Crisco on the stove at all times. She even added Crisco to bacon when she fried it and she never cleaned the skillet. She simply poured the grease down the drain when the skillet got too full.

When the old man died, I received six-hundred dollars from his insurance. Ellen only sent the check to me after I agreed to sign it over to her for his funeral. She said the funeral wasn't her responsibility and she had no obligation to pay for it. I was told that if I didn't sign the check over to her, she'd leave him at the funeral home and let them put him in a pauper's unmarked grave.

Some things you never forget.

Strange Children I Have Known

I have no doubt that anyone reading this has known some very strange people. But, I'm not sure if they have had the epiphany that strange people come from strange children.

I have known some very strange kids. Through all my years in school, I think I've known at least one kid in every grade who was extremely odd, bizarre, or just plain creepy.

Some were simply peculiar in their dress or their habits. Others developed an eccentric personality at a young age with all of the attending idiosyncrasies.

After careful consideration of all of them, however, a few have seared themselves into my memory because they did things that could never, in any way, shape, or form, be considered normal.

Here are some of the most memorable ones:

First, let's consider a kid I knew named Gary. He was a consummate pencil eater. Now, before you jump to any conclusions, thinking you know all about kids eating pencils, let me make it clear that Gary was unique in this activity and he could have turned professional. Gary didn't simply eat a pencil, he was systematic and efficient at it.

His pencil of choice was the *Ticonderoga Yellow No. 2 Pencil* manufactured by the Dixon company. Although he would chew on any pencil available in a pinch, he had a special preference for a brand new Ticonderoga Yellow No. 2.

I was fascinated by his culinary fondness for pencils and one day I gave him my full attention, watching him throughout the entire process, making mental notes as he ingested a pencil.

First, he would nibble on the entire pencil (like eating an ear of corn) breaking down the paint on the pencil. Next, he would return to the starting position and nibble off the cracked paint until nothing was left but the wood.

Having stripped the paint off, he then began at the tip of the pencil, nibbling off the wood. Sometimes he would hold the pencil in his mouth and let it soften with saliva to make it more chewy.

Returning to his "ear of corn" process, he would start at the tip and rotate the pencil, nibbling off the wood, until only the graphite was left. He carefully moved up the entire pencil, nibbling and swallowing until nothing was left except the bare graphite-clay core.

At this point, his technique required him to be exceedingly careful, lest he break the fragile piece of graphite. He would hold the metal ferrule that held the eraser and connected it to the pencil. He would carefully chew on the end of the ferrule until he worked the eraser out. He would chew on the eraser for quite sometime, making it last, as though it were a piece of chewing gum.

Having finished with the eraser, he worked the ferrule between his teeth until it was loosened and it could be slipped away from the small bit of wood under it. With the ferrule removed from the pencil, he used his front teeth to flatten it and then swallow it whole.

This left the graphite core and only a small bit of wood. He nibbled and ate the wood first. At last, nothing was left except for the long, slender graphite core.

At this point, he began eating the graphite as one might nibble away a candy cane. Starting at one end, he took just enough of the graphite in his teeth to bite and pulverize it. He kept at it until the entire piece of graphite was in his mouth.

It's funny that as I write this, the memory brings back some diminutive details which might seem insignificant, but really are interesting (at least to me). By the time Gary had eaten the whole pencil, his fingers, lips, and teeth were silvery and shiny from the graphite.

Gary's pencil eating routine lasted throughout the fourth grade. After that, I lost track of him and I have no idea what happened to him. For all I know, he may have become hard core. He may be out there somewhere eating a *Bic-Stic* or a *Paper-Mate* even as I write this.

Gary was a strange child.

Another kid I went to school with was named David. He had the habit of playing with his hair. He would grab about an inch wide swath of his hair and twirl it, pulling at the same time. Little by little, through the school, year I noticed that he was developing small bald spots all over his head.

Ever the inquisitive person, one day I asked him why he pulled his hair like that. His explanation was, "Shut up. It's none of your stupid business. You're stupid." I never questioned him about this compulsion again.

More disgusting than the hair pulling, was the fact that he would eat the hair he pulled out of his head. Over the years I've discovered that there are actual medical names for these habits. When I was a kid, we called things like this "habits." Today, they are referred to as "disorders."

The hair twirling and pulling disorder is called Trichotillomania. The hair eating disorder is called Trichophagia. The scientific community has yet to figure out why people do it.

By the time the school year was coming to an end, David's compulsive disorders had become apparent to everyone. With the exception of the little tufts of hair on his head, he was bald.

On the first day of the next school year, David was there. I think his parents and the teacher thought they had figured out a solution to his problem. His hair had all grown back, but he had a crew cut. I think they sent him to the barber twice a week because his hair never got long enough to twirl, pull, or eat.

David was a strange child.

I know that fingernail biting is a common habit, but one kid I knew, Frankie was his name, gave new meaning to the practice.

Frankie didn't just bite his fingernails, he destroyed them. One day, while we were sitting at a communal desk with some other children, I noticed his finger tips. They looked like the stubby little fingers you'd find on a gnome. There was very little left of his fingernails.

Frankie's "Onychophagia" was so severe that only about a quarter of in inch of fingernail was left on every finger on his hands. He really worked at it. Literally, all that remained of his fingernails were covering the quick on every finger. I wondered how long it would be before he started digging his fingernails out of the roots.

Another habit Frankie had was to sneak up behind an unsuspecting kid and pound him in the back of the head with his fist, yelling, "Ya wanna fight, ya sonavabitch?"

Frankie was strange and belligerent.

Another kid I knew was named Jimmy. The problem with Jimmy was that he was a "mouth breather." Simply put, Jimmy either could not, or would not, breath through his nose. In my school days, guys like this were referred to as "slack-jawed," meaning their jaws hung loose, as though they were on a broken hinge.

Anyone who has ever watched the character "Cletus" on *The Simpsons* television show can appreciate the meaning of slack-jawed and mouth-breather. Although there is no scientific evidence to prove the hypothesis, slack-jawed mouth-breathers are commonly considered to be stupid, ignorant hillbillies.

It was irritating, to say the least, to sit next to Jimmy because mouth breathers inhale and exhale much more laboriously than nose breathers. When it was quiet in the classroom, Jimmy's breathing could be heard by everyone.

Jimmy also had a bizarre way of talking. Whenever he got excited, he would get overly flustered and forget the word he was trying to say. He'd blurt out something extremely unexpected.

One day in particular that I recall, Jimmy was in front of the class giving a book report. He wasn't very good in front of people and he began to panic. He was telling a story about someone driving a car and he was trying to say, " . . . pressed the gas pedal." What came out was, " . . . he pushed from the top to the bottom on the autocar's foot throttle." Then he began to giggle and he couldn't stop. The teacher finally took pity on him, thanked him for his report, and told him to sit down.

Jimmy wasn't the strangest kid I knew, but he was still pretty darned strange.

I find it unfortunate that the next story is actually a continuation of the "David story." I wish I could say that his problems were eradicated by keeping his hair cut short, but sadly, that is not the case.

Once he had been shorn of his locks and having nothing to twirl, pull, or eat, he was still a child with a compulsive need for bad habits. He surpassed himself with his next venture. He began to eat his own boogers.

I was sitting quietly at my desk one day reading a book about Enos Slaughter. For those of you who don't know who Enos Slaughter was, he played baseball for the Saint Louis Cardinals. He's famous for the "Slaughter Mad Dash" when he ran from first base to home plate on a fly ball to centerfield. Slaughter had more hustle on an off day than Pete Rose had in a whole year. You can look it up.

Anyway, when I looked up and saw David poking his finger in his nose, digging around, and pulling out a big, green, stretchy booger. He didn't simply eat it, he looked at it, sniffed it, and then put it in his mouth, pulling it off his finger with his two front teeth. I almost puked.

After class I went to the teacher, gave her all the gory details, and requested that I be moved to another seat, as far away from "Booger Boy" as possible. She let out a big sigh, gave me a frustrated look, and said she would see what could be done about it.

Apparently I wasn't the only kid in the

room who had seen this and who wanted to be as far away from him as possible. The teacher changed the seating arrangements so that David was put in a chair by himself in the back, behind all the other students. This way no one could see him, as if anyone wanted to.

An additional problem developed with David's nose. He often picked his nose so fiercely it began to bleed and he often spent a lot of time in the school nurse's office.

One positive outcome from all this was that when I was moved to another seat, I ended up sitting next to a very cute little girl.

After that school year, I have no idea what happened to David because he never came back to our school. By that time, however, his unconventional behavior had left its indelible mark on me. His hair and booger compulsions had burned their images into my little mind.

I have investigated this "booger" compulsion and discovered that the eating of boogers is given the name mucophagy.

Believe it or not, an Austrian doctor says eating boogers is good for children. He claims the "dead germ corpses" (known to common folks like you and me as boogers) reinforces the immune system. He equates boogers to a nasal penicillin and tells parents to encourage their children to eat their boogers.

Not only do I think David was a very strange child, I think the Austrian doctor is exceptionally strange, if not just plain nuts.

There's one kid I'm going to mention here that might need a chapter of his own, but I'm going to keep his story short because thinking of him makes me angry. I don't even know his name.

For some reason that escapes my memory, Mama had taken me with her to the home of some people she knew. I think she worked with the woman in the Esther Baptist Church.

Mama was in the kitchen talking with the woman. I was sitting on their couch minding my business. The woman's little kid, about my age, maybe six, came into the room. He never said a word. He just walked up behind me and bashed me on the head with his cap gun, opening a gash that quickly started bleeding.

I was on the verge of beating the daylights out of him when Mama came in, picked me up, put a handkerchief on my head, and told me I shouldn't hit him back because, "He's not right in the head."

The kid's mother never bothered to correct him and she never bothered to say, "Sorry." She just ignored the whole episode. She grabbed his hand, took him to the kitchen, and told him to sit in a chair.

At that moment, I learned one of life's little lessons. Oddballs are given a pass when it comes to being responsible for their actions. I didn't agree with it when I was six and I still don't agree with it. Even if the kid was retarded, he had no right to do what he did and he should have been punished. I can imagine the kind of things he got away with because he was "different."

That was one strange kid.

I'm in the front. David Rasche is on the right. Harold is behind Linda Rasche. I think this may be the neighborhood Cub Scout Troop.

Grandma Was A Joiner

As I sat here and wrote the title to this story I realized I may have given the wrong impression of Grandma. Let me clarify the issue. Grandma was not a joiner in the woodworking sense. She enjoyed joining clubs. She was a member of almost every club, lodge, and association in the Lead Belt area.

Now I suppose I should also clarify the term "Lead Belt," which refers to the lead mining district in southeastern Missouri.

Philip Francois Renault came here from France in 1719, did extensive explorations, and he started lead mining operations in 1720. Sainte Genevieve was founded as a river port for lead exports and Moses Austin initiated large-scale mining and smelting at Potosi.

My hometown, Flat River, was surrounded by other small towns, such as Esther, Elvins, Rivermines, Leadwood, Desloge, Bonne Terre, Bismark, Doe Run, and Knob Lick.

Grandma was born and reared in Bismark. Grandpa came from Irondale. They moved to Flat River in the 1930s and bought a house there. They both died in that house.

The house is still there. I wonder if the people living in it today realize that it has quite a history. It was originally built and owned by the St. Joe Lead Company as were all the houses on that street. It was, indeed, a "company house."

When Grandpa and Grandma bought the house its address was 9Y Theodore Street. Prior to that, the street was referred to as "Silk Stocking Row" because only the company big shots living in the houses could afford silk stockings. In those days, company houses were quite similar to the "company store" referred to in the old song "Sixteen Tons."

I can't seem to help myself. I'm always getting off subject. Back to the story of Grandma and her affiliations.

As a young girl in Bismark, Grandma became a member of *Rainbow Girls*, the juvenile lodge of the *Daughters of the Eastern Star*. When she was old enough, she graduated to *The Order of the Eastern Star,* the female counterpart of the *Masonic Lodge*. Grandma's father was a Mason and she carried on the tradition. Grandpa was also a Mason and an Odd Fellow.

In addition to the *Order of the Eastern Star*, Grandma was a member in good standing in the *Daughters of Rebekah*, the female counterpart of the *Independent Order of Odd Fellows*.

If that weren't enough, just to keep busy, she was also a member of the *Pythian Sisters*, the female auxiliary of the *Knights of Pythias*; and a *Daughter of the American Revolution*; and a *Daughter of Union Civil War Veterans*. She qualified for the *DUCV* because her father, Andrew Jackson Wallace was a union soldier (a blacksmith) in the Civil War.

On occasion, Grandma would entertain us with stories about a relative further in the past who she claimed was with General Washington at the time of the Delaware Crossing. Although I have a picture of her father wearing a medal from the Civil War, I have no proof corroborating the Revolutionary War stories.

You must understand that Grandma wasn't just a member of these lodges. She invariably held an important, key position in these organizations. She was, in today's vernacular, "A Player." She was heavily involved in each and every lodge to which she belonged. She held exalted titles such as *Worshipful Mistress*, *Worthy Master*, *Secretary*, *Treasurer*, *Overseer*, *Gatekeeper*, *Chaplain*, and many others I'm unable to recall. She was, to say the least, a "big shot" in all of her lodges.

I, myself, was a member of the *Order of DeMolay* during my teen years and later a Mason although I haven't been active for many, many years. I am, however, active in the *Patrons of Husbandry*, commonly known as The Grange.

Where was I? Where is this all going? Oh, yes, I remember now.

My brother, Harold, played the accordion. He was never good enough to qualify for a pinky ring, but at least the songs he played were recognizable. He was especially good with toe-tapping tunes such as *Lady of Spain* and *In Country Gardens*. Because of his musical talents, he was often the "entertainment" at many of Grandma's lodge assemblages.

The unfortunate element in this sad little tale of woe was that Grandma never considered it feasible that I should stay at home when she and Harold were out-and-about among the local luminaries. I would have preferred to stay home with Grandpa and watch the *Gillette Friday Night Fights* but Grandma pretty well ruled the roost. It may even be appropriate to refer to her as a "hard woman" in this respect.

I was put into my little navy blue suit, my white shirt with French cuffs and cuff-links, my pre-knotted tie, and I was dragged unwillingly to these festive occasions.

It might not have been so bad if I had been allowed to be part of the entertainment. I readily admit to being quite the "ham." It's been said that if you shine a flashlight on me I'll "do five minutes." It was problematical, however, that Harold was never able to learn to play any of the songs I liked to sing. So he played and I sat.

I can envision the entire scene just like it was yesterday. Grandma and all the other lodge ladies in their finest dresses with fresh, blue hairdos, heavy makeup, and a quart or two of perfume, decked out in their special sashes, belts, and caps. I see them marching around the room, performing their intricate maneuvers while Harold is pounding out a jerky rendition of *In Country Gardens*.

The pounding of a gavel, the reading of

minutes, reports of community activities, and secret, memorized rituals. More clandestine handshakes, silent secret signs, dramatized oaths, and glorified affirmations.

Ah, yes, heady stuff, indeed.

Trying out my new bike on the Emerson Elementary School playground. I don't remember the little girl, but I'm always ready to help a lady needing a ride.

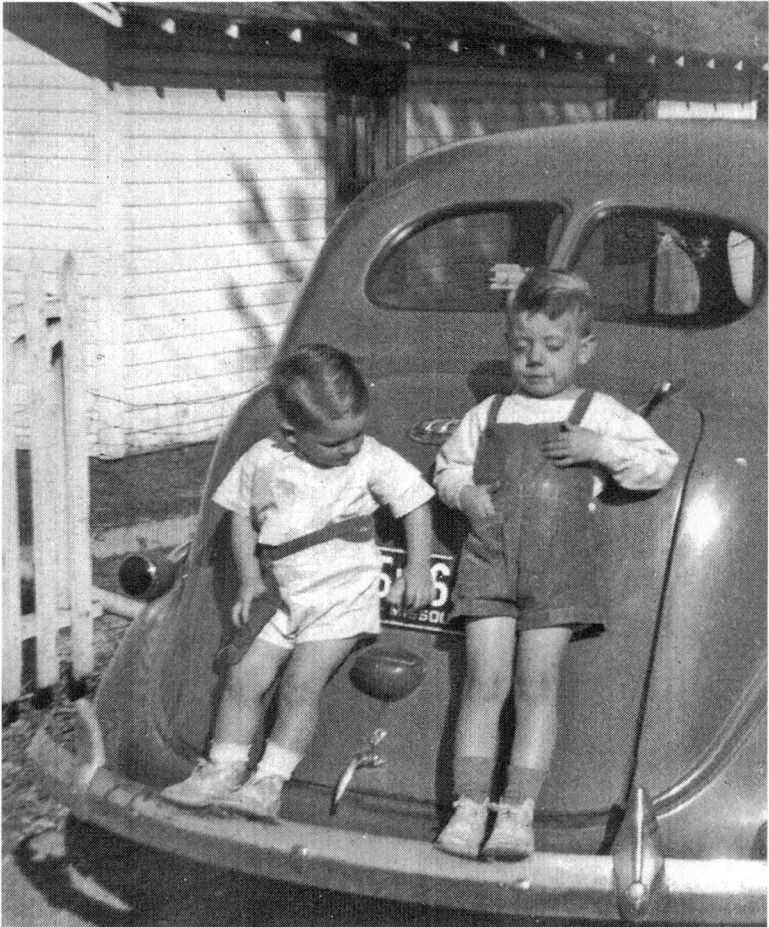

Grand-Daddy Criteser's 1937 Plymouth.
I could swear those are bullet holes in
the rear split-window. After all, I was
packing heat that day.

Shaking The Family Tree

After giving this a great deal of thought, I've come to the conclusion that it's difficult to make a "family tree" interesting. Actions, events, and personalities surrounding the people in the family tree, of course, make for good story telling, but names, birth dates, death dates, and marriage dates make up nothing more than a "list."

So, admitting this right up front, I'm going to go through the birthing, dying, and begatting as quickly as possible to get to the real subject of this story: Grandpa Province.

The furthest information I can find on my ancestors goes back to a fellow named John Lafayette Province. He was born about 1771 in Powell Valley, Tennessee and he died between 1812 and 1862. I know that's a very long "in between" but it's the best information available. John married a gal named Lizzie Jordan who was born around 1775 and died between 1812 and 1870. Another very long "in between" but I have to use what I have to work with. John and Lizzie had the following children:

Peggy Province
Hannah Province
Henry Province
Herman Province
William Province

Louis Province
Joseph Province

Joseph Province, the baby of the family, was born on the 21st of January, 1809 in Nashville, Tennessee and he died on the 27th of March, 1876 in Irondale, Missouri. He married Rutha Ann Forshee in Monroe County, Tennessee around 1832. Rutha Ann was born on the 10th of September, 1811 in Nashville. She died on the 28th of August, 1902. Joseph and Rutha had the following children:

Martha Jane Province
John Anderson Province
William Lafayette Province
Margaret Isabel Province
Mary E. Province
James Richard Province
Joseph Elbert Province
Lucy Province

William Lafayette Province was born on the 9th of May, 1838 in Irondale, Missouri and he died there on the 4th of February, 1917. Great-Grandpa William married a woman named Edna Elizabeth Robinson on the 4th of August, 1858. The marriage took place in Silver Mines, Missouri. Edna was the daughter of John Robinson and Lavinia McMurtury. She was born on the 23rd of October, 1839 and she died on the 7th of September, 1870. She was only thirty-one when she passed away and I've never been able to find out what it was that killed her.

William and Edna had six children that lived. They were:

Joseph Monroe Province
John Lafayette Province
Martha Alice Province
William Henry Province
Edna Ann Province
Lucy Arminta Province

Two years and one month after Edna's death, on the 23rd of November, 1872 to be exact, William re-married. His second wife was Mariah Means, who was born on the 11th of November, 1851. She was the daughter of David Means and Marie Bower. She died on the 11th of June, 1943. William and Mariah had eleven children that lived. They were:

Laura June Province
Barbara Collinzia Province
Charles Oman Province
Francis Alonzo Province
Iola Lillian Province
Rosa Mariah Province
David Seaborne Province
Marion Lee Province
George Luther Province
Thomas Emery Province
James Cleveland Province
Eliza Eugenia Province

Marion Lee Province, my Grandpa, was born on the 14th of February, 1886 in Irondale and he died on the 19th of February, 1975 in Flat River. He was number 14 out of 18 children sired by Great-Grandpa Province.

Simply typing in the names of all these ancestors has just about worn me out. I can imagine how my female forebears must have felt popping out all these kids and having to take care of them. Of course back then, they all lived on farms and the kids were kept busy.

Grandpa, of course, had a small clan of his own. He married Alice Bisby Wallace from Bismark, Missouri, which is about three miles from Irondale.

I have very little in the way of verifiable records about Grandma Province other than some old photographs. She claimed to be a relative of two famous people; one was General Lew Wallace, the author of *Ben-Hur*, and the other was Scotland's William Wallace, known today as *Braveheart*.

As I've said, I'm unable to verify any of this, but I'm sure Grandma would never prevaricate. She was, to say the least, a woman to be reckoned with. Grandpa and Grandma Province had five children a number of grand-children. They were:

Marion Sylvester Province
(Married Jennie Eldridge)
    Alice Province
    John Province
Theresa Province
(Married Herman Chamberlain)
    Nelda Chamberlain
    Mary Chamberlain
Herman Harold Province, Sr.
(Married Helen Marguerite Criteser)
    Deloros Ray Province
    Freddie Lee Province

Herman Harold Province, Jr.
Charles Michael Province
Lena Province
(Married Ralph Cross)
   Glen Cross
   Kay Cross
Euluan Province
(Married Ola Violet Lindsey)
   Coral Province
   Edward Province
   Nikki Province

Herman Harold Province, Sr. was my father. He married Helen Marguerite Criteser on the 29th of September, 1930 and their first child, a girl, died immediately after birth. The three subsequent children were boys.

Back to Grandpa, who never talked much, but when he did, it was through idoms, colloquialisms, and witty little sayings; Things like:

Even a blind hog finds an acorn once in a while.
Politicians are all as crooked as a dog's hind leg.
It's rainin' like a cow pissin' on a flat rock.
He's as strong as a little French horse.
I'm so hungry I could eat a seventy-five cent plate.
He's so happy he could kiss his mother-in-law.
If a horse raises his tail, move to the side.

Sometimes I had no idea what he was talking about, but he was always entertaining. Although Grandpa was known for his reticence, he would occasionally regale me with stories that his father had told to him.

151

Great-Grandpa William, for example, refused to join either army during the War of Northern Aggression, although his personal philosophy tended to lean toward the Rebel cause. He was a man who thought people should be left alone and left to their own devices. He held the firm conviction that government, any government, was inherently evil.

One of Grandpa's favorite stories was about a man named Sam Hildebrand who became one of the best known Rebel Guerillas and Yankee killers in Missouri.

If you've ever heard the stories about Jesse James, about him being a "Robin Hood" type of guy, forget them; they're nothing but lies. Jesse James was a murderer, a thief, and a crook. He never stole anything he didn't keep for himself and he would drop the hammer on anyone who got in his way without the slightest hint of remorse.

The stories that Hollywood made up about Jesse James should actually be attributed to Sam Hildebrand.

Sam just wanted to be left alone. He wanted no part of either side of the war, but one fateful day, some Yankees came to his farm, stole his hogs and horses, killed his wife and brother, and burned his house.

Like any man of principle, that made Sam angry and it turned him against the Yankees. Right then and there, he began his personal, private guerilla war against the "blue-bellies."

A number of books have been written

about Sam, so I won't go into a lot of detail here. Suffice it to say that Sam's vendetta against the Yankees was violent, brutal, and vicious. Sam was not a man to be trifled with.

According to Grandpa, Sam was on the run and the Yankees were hot on his trail. He was on the way to his hideout in the bluffs overlooking Big River near the Bonne Terre mines and he stopped by Great-Grandpa William's farm. Sam and William were friends so William hid Sam under an old hog trough and he began to groom Sam's horse, acting like it was his.

When the Yankees came riding into William's yard, trampling everything in their path, he was informed that, "The U.S. Cavalry is searching for a miscreant named Sam Hildebrand." William said he never heard of the fellow.

The Yankee captain then "confiscated" the horse William was grooming, claiming the U.S. Army needed it more than he did. Luckily William had a special picketing place for his horses, hidden in the woods about a mile away, so the Yankees couldn't find any other horses to steal.

As the soldiers left William's yard, the captain threatened William, warning him that if he found out where Sam was and he didn't turn him in, they'd come back, burn his house, and hang him.

William thanked the kind gentleman for his benevolence and consideration, turned on his heel, and walked into his house. He grabbed his guns, hid behind the door, and waited to see if the Yankees were going to break into his house.

The soldiers must have been in a charitable mood that day because they left the yard and continued their hunt for Mr. Hildebrand.

Much later, after it had been dark for a while, Sam crawled out from under the hog trough and was preparing to leave when Great-Grandpa William told him where his horse pickets were and told Sam he could take one of them. Sam thanked him for his kindness and left. Great-Grandpa William never saw Sam again.

Another of Grandpa's stories went like this:

In the 1820s, Grandpa's Great-Grandpa, John Lafayette Province, went fishing. He was minding his own business when he noticed a half-dozen Indians riding along the crest of a ridge about a half-mile away.

When the Indians saw him, they stopped, dismounted, and sat in front of their horses, watching him.

Nothing happened for a while but after John had caught a mess of catfish, he started to gather his belongings for the trip home. All he had with him was his fishing gear, his horse, his knife, and his old single-shot musket.

When the Indians saw him preparing to leave, they mounted their horses and rode toward him. He had a bad feeling about the whole affair, especially since he was heavily outnumbered. He figured the best thing to do was to just stand still and see what they wanted.

Well, what they wanted, apparently, was every damn thing he owned. Without saying a word, they rode up, took his horse, his musket, his knife, and (adding insult to injury) his mess of catfish.

He stood there and watched them ride off with everything except the clothes on his back and he felt lucky they didn't take them, too. Had he protested, they would have killed him.

Shaking his head, he realized that they had waited to rob him until he had caught a mess of catfish for them.

Okay, one more Grandpa story and then I'll stop:

This story concerns immigrants brought in by the St. Joe Lead Company just prior to the First World War.

The immigrants we're talking about here were from the Slavic area of Europe; Bohemia, Hungary, Rumania, Batavia, and places that were at one time part of the old Hapsburg Empire. This was when Kaiser Wilhelm was the big shot in Germany.

As it was told to me, after the start of World War I and things were getting pretty nasty over there, some people in the United States wanted to send American soldiers to help the British and the French. (Boy, does that sound familiar.)

According to Grandpa, one of the "Bo-Hunks" made the mistake of telling a miner that after all the Americans were drafted and off to war, he and his fellow "Hunkies" would have all the women and jobs to themselves. A further mistake was that he was laughing as he said it.

That was the wrong thing to say to these guys. They gathered a large group of their biggest guys, herded the immigrants down to the railroad station, beat the living hell out of them, and put them on a train, telling them that if they came back, they'd be killed. And they meant it.

Grandpa added that in addition to making dim-witted remarks about taking away the American's jobs and women, the "Hunkies" were also threatening the small advances being made by the newly organized miner's union.

Research I did on this story has confirmed its veracity.

According to Grandpa, the "Bo-Hunks" were stupid and they'd work for beer instead of a paycheck.

I can testify to the fact that Grandpa was a hard case. He was tough as nails, stood straight as a railroad track, and he laughed like a blacksmith's bellows. Grandpa was a damn good guy.

Upon reflection, I think he was probably more of a father to me than my old man ever was, even if he did take the razor strap to me on occasion.

Pictures of the Province Family

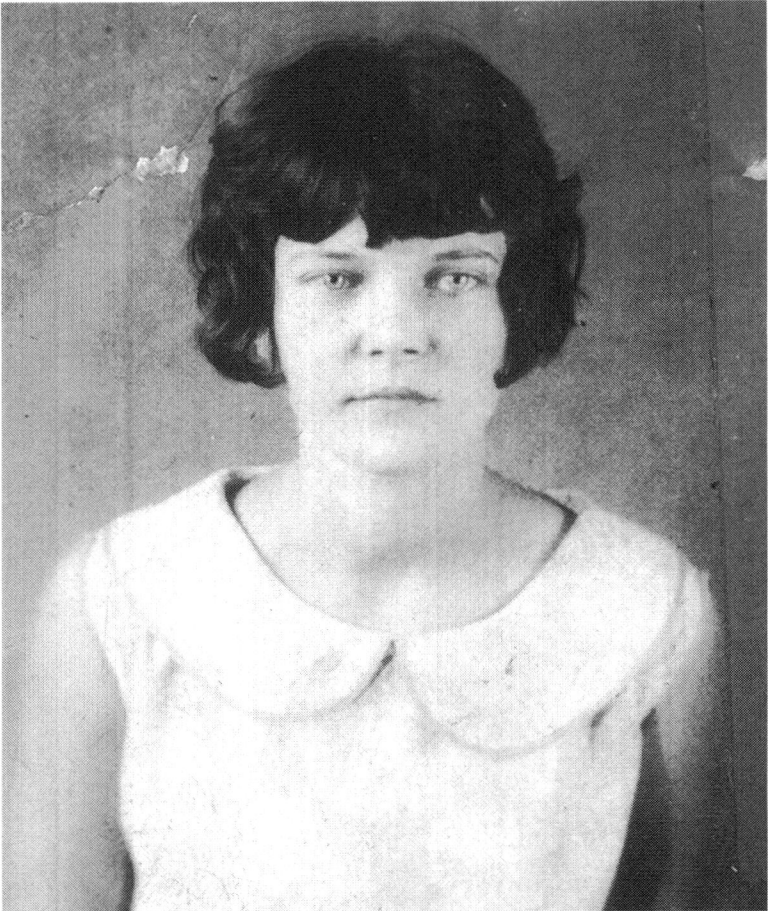

Mama's yearbook picture when she
was a junior in High School.

Mama on Graduation Day, 1929.
A fountain pen broke open on this
picture and I had to rebuild
the whole top half.

Mama and Freddie Lee, around 1940.
He was happy when he had
Mama all to himself.

Helen Marguerite Criteser
"Mama"

Mama with Freedie Lee, 1932.

Esther graduating class of 1929.
The old man is in the front row, sixth from the left with the jazzy pants.
Mama is in the third row tenth from the right with the black collar pen.

Herman H. Province, Sr. around 1929.
AKA "The Old Man."

Herman H. Province, Sr. around 1953.
This picture was taken for a book about
Flat River, Missouri when he was mayor.

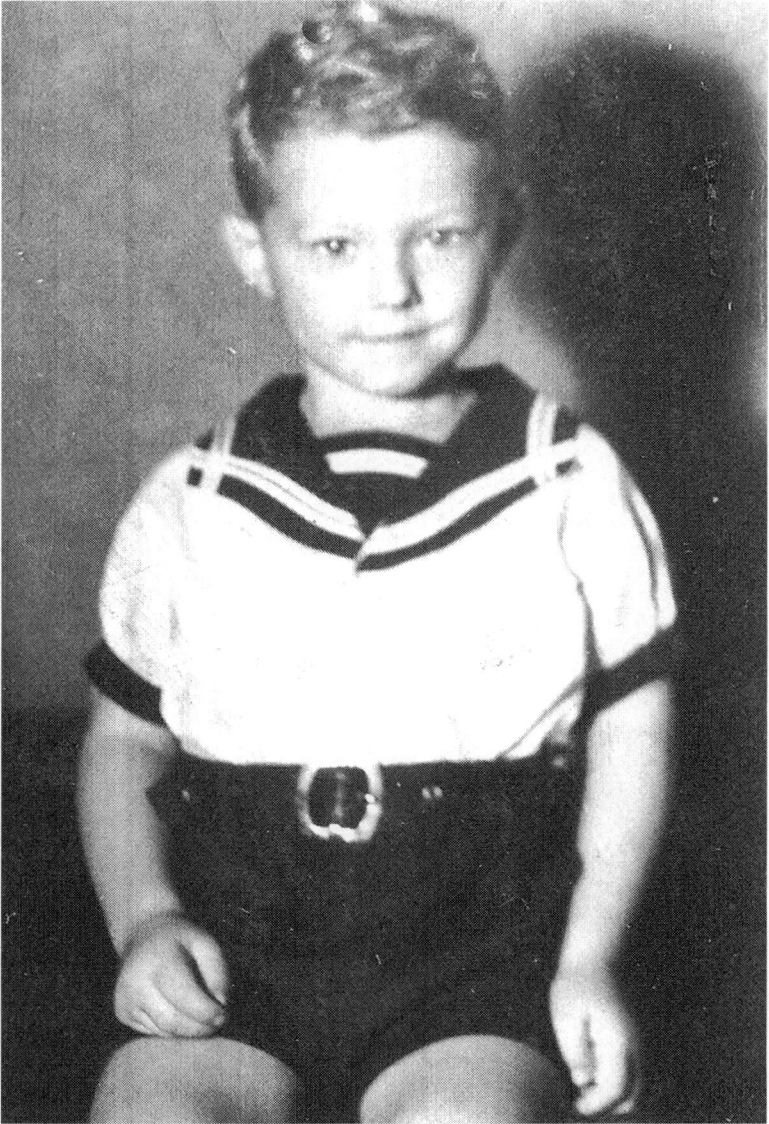

Freddie Lee Province around 1937.
He would have been about five or six.

Freddie around 1949. This would have been
about the time he graduated and joined
the Army. He was in the 82nd Airborne.

Herman Harold Province, Jr., 1942.

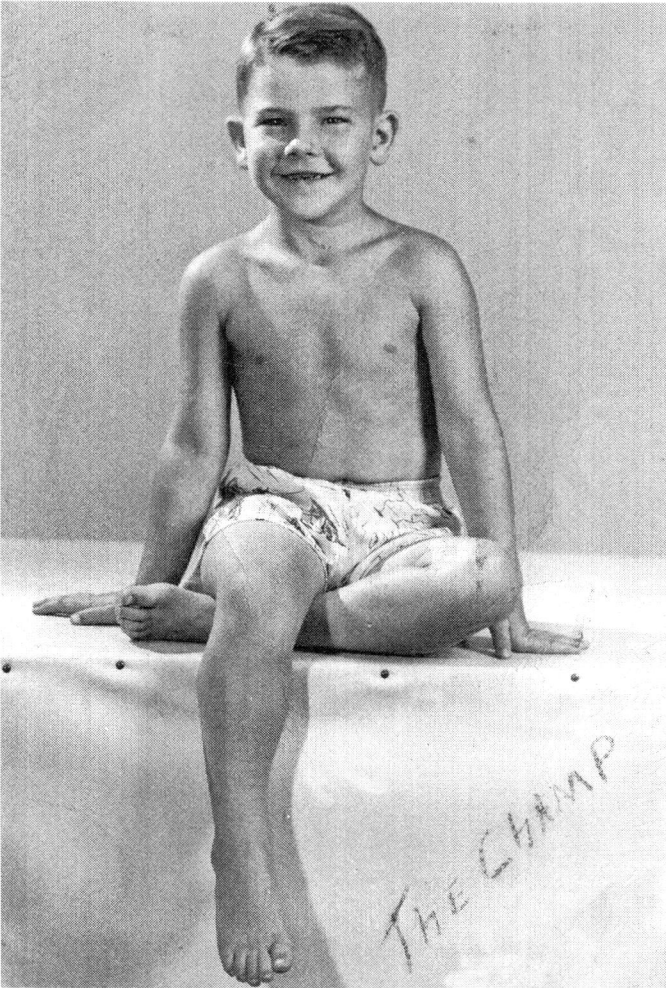

I have no idea why I wrote
"The Champ" on this picture.
It must have very warm that
day since I'm almost naked.

Freddie Lee Province in the back.
Herman Harold Province, Jr. on the left.
Charles Michael Province on the right.

Grandkids
Back row from the left:
Alice (Uncle Marian's daughter) is holding me.
Nelda (Aunt Theresa's daughter), Freddie Lee,
and Glen (Aunt Lema's son).
Front row from left:
Kay (Aunt Lema's daughter) and Harold.

The Province Family, 1945.
Me, Harold, Mama, Daddy, and Freddie Lee.

The whole clan. I think we were having a day at the river or some such thing. Left to right: Freddie Lee, The old man, Harold, Mama, and me. Around 1947.

Grandmother Criteser

Grand-daddy Criteser

Grandmother and Grand-daddy Criteser. To her left is their 1936 Plymouth. Behind him is the rally, old garage and our 1935 Ford.

Grandma and Grandpa in 1934. I don't
know the grandkids, but Grandpa's mother
is in the chair (Maria Means Province).

Grandpa and Grandma Province.
I think this was taken for their 50th
Wedding Anniversary, about 1956.

Grandpa and Grandma Province
probably at some family wedding.

Grandpa, Grandma, and their kids:
Left to right: Aunt Lema, Uncle Euluen,
Herman, Uncle Marian, and Aunt Theresa.

The last picture of Grandpa, Grandma and
their kids; Left to right: Uncle Marian,
Aunt Theresa, Uncle Euluen,
Herman, and Aunt Lema.

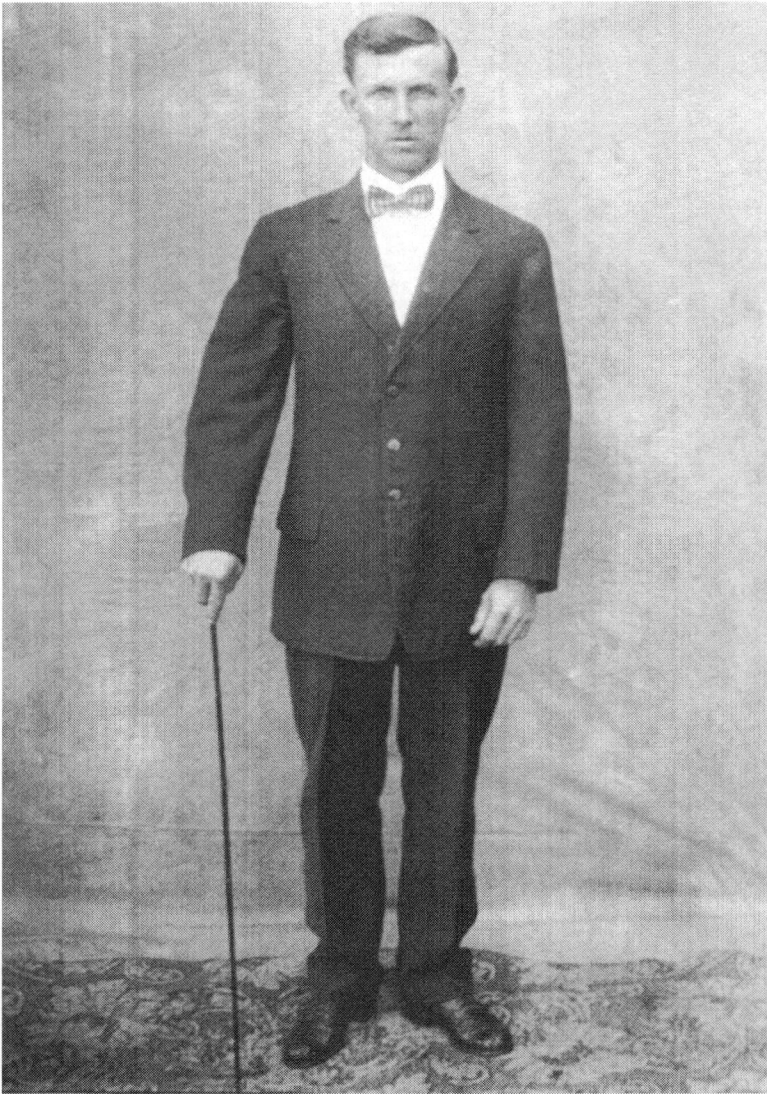

Marian Lee Province
aka Grandpa Province
1886-1975

Alice Bisby Wallace
aka Grandma Province
1889-1969

Grandpa's and Grandma's kids
when they were in High School.
L-R (rear): Euluen, Marian, Theresa.
L-R (front): My old man, Lema.

L-R: Front; Nikki, Grandpa & Glen, John, Grandma, Eddie.
Standing; Mama (holding Harold), Daddy, Uncle Euluan,
Freddie, Aunt Ola, Uncle Marian, Aunt Lema, Aunt Jennie,
Uncle Ralph, Aunt Theresa, Uncle Herman, Coral, Alice,
and Nelda. Mama was pregnant with me in this picture.

Andrew Jackson Wallace and
Frances Caroline Wilson Wallace,
probably around 1880. Frances
was Andrew's second wife.

Great Grandpa Andrew Jackson Wallace
and Frances Coraline Wilson Wallace.
My Grandma Province's parents.
He's wearing his "Grand Army of the
Republic" medal from the Civil War.
He was a damn Yankee.

Frances Coraline Wilson Wallace
Grandma Province's Mother
A few years after the Civil War

Frances Coraline Wilson Wallace
Grandma Province's Mother
Around 1915

Amanda Clementine Wallace
Grandma Province's Sister
1878-1949

Lucinda Wallace
Grandma Province's Sister
1886-1968

Ulysses Grant Wallace
Grandma Province's Brother
1883-1957

Christopher Columbus Wallace
Grandma Province's Half-Brother
1872-1953
and
Catherine Jane King, his wife

Andrew Jackson Wallace's children:
Left to right: Christopher Columbus Wallace,
Amanda Clementine Wallace, Ulysses Grant
Wallace, Lucinda Wallace, and Alice Bisby
Wallace Province (my Grandma).

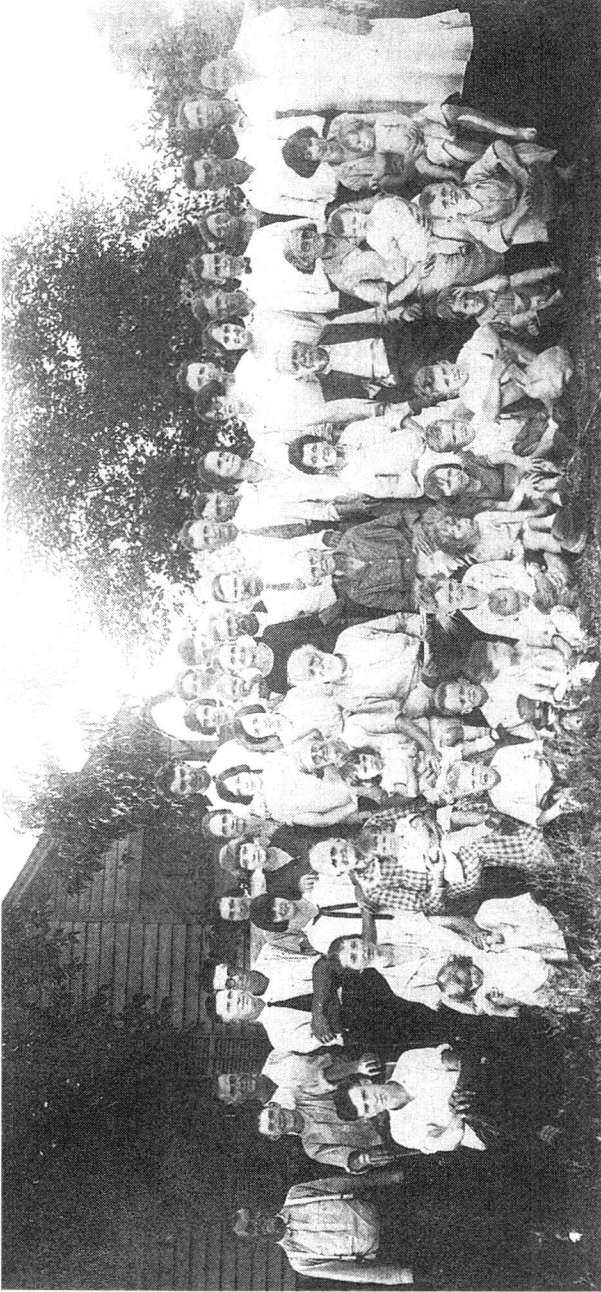

A small Province family reunion, probably around 1930. Grandpa and Grandma are on the far right. Other aunts and uncles are in various places in the group. The row of old folks sitting down were all born in the 1840s or 1850s.

Charles M. Craving

45406686R00114

Made in the USA
San Bernardino, CA
07 February 2017